THE MARRIAGE EXPERIENCE

*Weekly Conversation Starters to Build
the Relationship You Desire*

RYAN & JENNY BROWN

ENCOURAGE
PUBLISHING
NEW ALBANY, INDIANA

Cover design: Ryan Brown

Interior design: Jonathan Lewis

Editing: Leslie Turner

Published and printed in the United States of America for worldwide distribution.

Library of Congress Control Number: 2022938523

Cataloguing data:

Brown, Ryan C. and Jennifer M.

The Marriage Experience: Weekly Conversation Starters to Build the Relationship You Desire

1. Persuasion (Psychology) 2. Marriage (Sociology) 3. The Christian Life (Religion—Philosophy) 4. Christian Living—Love and marriage 5. Christian Living—Spiritual growth 6. Christian Living—Personal growth

Dewey decimal classification: 248: Christian experience, practice, life

Unless otherwise stated all Scripture quotations by Jenny Brown are taken from The Holy Bible, New International Version®, NIV®. Copyright © 1973, 1978, 1984, 2011 by Biblica, Inc.® Used by permission of Zondervan. All rights reserved worldwide. The "NIV" and "New International Version" are trademarks registered in the United States Patent and Trademark Office by Biblica, Inc.®

Unless otherwise stated all Scripture quotations by Ryan Brown are taken from the ESV® Bible (The Holy Bible, English Standard Version®). Copyright © 2001 by Crossway, a publishing ministry of Good News Publishers.. Used by permission. All rights reserved.

The Marriage Experience [softcover, eBook] ISBN 978-1-7343231-4-6

The Marriage Experience [hardcover] ISBN 978-1-7343231-1-5

Published by: Encourage Publishing, New Albany, Indiana, www.encouragepublishing.com

CONTENTS

FOREWORD

Brad and Marilyn Rhoads
Co-founders of *Grace Marriage* and
featured experts on Focus on the Family

AFTER YEARS OF WORKING with churches of virtually every denomination, after having the opportunity to serve thousands of couples through our combined roles as attorney, author, marriage pastor, counselor, and as co-founders of *Grace Marriage*, we know two things that are paramount in a relationship: regular and ongoing communication, and consistent, deep, emotional and spiritual intimacy.

Ryan and Jenny Brown understand this connection, and in *The Marriage Experience* they have provided a great pathway for couples to communicate and draw closer to each other. We are so thankful to call them friends and have had the privilege of watching them model these two vital elements in their own marriage. God has shown them how to stay connected and grow together. Their marriage ministry flows from this experience, and now we are blessed by the way they share those insights and personal stories in this book.

The pursuit of intimacy and oneness is a journey worth taking. As you grow in mutual vulnerability and understanding, the enjoyment you experience in your marriage will skyrocket. You find the joy of getting to do life with your very best friend. You go through the highs and the lows together and, through the process, your hearts will become intricately intertwined in a beautiful and God-glorifying way.

Unfortunately, the busyness of life and destructive communication patterns create a roadblock for many couples. Some of us were discouraged early in life from sharing our emotions, or did not grow up with a healthy model of emotional communication. For others, our busy lives have allowed us to avoid deep and meaningful communication.

Whatever the reason, many couples end up rushing *through* life together instead of enjoying relationship *in* life together. Ryan and Jenny desire to help you remove those roadblocks. Intimacy and connection do not typically just happen organically. It takes intentionality and structure to build your relationship, which is where this book is so valuable. It guides you through conversations you probably would otherwise never have.

Many couples can go years talking about the day-to-day challenges of life, but miss out on really knowing each other. Now, we get it—these conversations can feel awkward. However, breaking through mere surface-level communication into heart intimacy is worth it.

Having worked with so many couples, we can see when two people are really experiencing the deep intimacy of marriage God intended. You can sense a comradery, a closeness, and, yes, a beauty to the relationship. You can actually feel the closeness when you are around a couple that is genuinely *experiencing* their marriage. They understand each other. They get each other. They are well positioned to effectively love each other.

Ryan and Jenny want you to experience life together in this way. They don't want any couple to just settle for side-by-side shallowness. Their prayer is that the depth you gain through this book puts you on a journey to become more loving, more generous, more sacrificial, and, most importantly, that the beauty of God is put on display through your marriage.

So, as you enjoy this book, take your time. Allow life to slow down so you can experience each other, and experience your marriage. Don't rush through this as another item on your to-do list. See it as a beautiful opportunity to enjoy and know the love of your life.

Our prayer for you is

- that you would enjoy connecting with each other on a deeper level;
- that Christ would get much glory through your marriage;
- that your marriage would stand out like a light on a hill; and
- that your marriage would be magnetic and God would use it for his purposes.

Hebrews 13:4 tells us "Let marriage be held in honor among all" (ESV). Reading this book and working on your own marriage is much bigger than you realize. Yes, it helps your relationship, but even more importantly, it exalts Christ and his creation of marriage.

Brad and Marilyn Rhoads

[Brad and Marilyn Rhoads are the founders of Gracemarriage.com, *a dual-purpose marriage ministry supporting local church marriage ministries and working directly with couples through their online platform and marriage community. They have helped thousands of couples across more than two decades and have an extensive speaking ministry in addition to their online platform.*

Grace Marriage *assists churches in changing marriage within the church and the culture at large through marriage retreats, marriage wellness materials, leadership training, and quarterly marriage groups.* GraceMarriage@ Home *works directly with couples, providing small group and online tools, resources, and a marriage-strengthening community. Brad and Marilyn were married in 1996 and have five children. Learn more about the Rhoads and their ministry at* gracemarriage.com.*]*

WELCOME!

WE ARE THRILLED THAT you have your hands on a project that was birthed from a love for marriage and a longing to give married couples space to connect on a deeper level in their relationship.

Did you know that your marriage has a purpose beyond your own personal fulfillment and companionship, as important as that is? We certainly did not understand this at the beginning of our relationship. A healthy, happy marriage not only brings lasting love and fulfillment to you and your family but also strengthens your understanding of God. Beyond that, your marriage, both in sacrifice and in strength, puts on display the relationship between Jesus and his bride, the church. Understanding this truth was a game-changer for us as we watched Christian marriages around us fall apart at the same pace as secular marriages.

Therefore, we intend for this book to be more than words on a screen or page, more than a box to check off your list. This is meant to be an *experience*. A *Jesus*-centered experience. A *gospel*-centered experience. Your time together, guided by this book, is meant to be an experience of the mind, body, and soul that will strengthen and draw you closer together, and closer to God.

We designed this series in four separate twelve-week units, all four closing with suggestions for an enjoyable celebration activity. Make each week's time a priority; deflect interruptions. But, **if you are unable to complete a week, do not skip it. Pick up where you left off as soon as you are able.**

Deepening your own marriage experience is a lifetime journey, well worth your continued effort.

Let's start the conversation!

WHO IS *THE MARRIAGE EXPERIENCE* FOR?

THE MARRIAGE EXPERIENCE IS for marriages in all seasons. Whether you've been married for four weeks, four years, or four decades, we truly believe what you experience here can and should deepen your marriage. It is never too late to create a growing, thriving connection for you and your spouse.

Have you been married a short period of time? You likely don't have a regular rhythm of communication yet. You may be juggling new life together, new jobs, perhaps growing a family, and may feel like you are just surviving. Be encouraged! Your intentionality now will serve you well for the rest of your life together.

Have you been married a long period of time? You probably already have a regular rhythm of life, but your marriage may not include this kind of connection with your spouse. This experience might be uncomfortable. You may have to sacrifice something for it to be effective. Be encouraged! Your sacrifice will hold lasting meaning for your spouse and will produce ongoing fruit in your marriage if you commit yourselves to it.

You might feel your marriage is already as strong as it can be, or perhaps you have convinced yourselves that nothing will change. Be encouraged! You picked up this book for a reason. We truly believe your marriage relationship is constantly moving, never stagnant. You are headed in the right direction!

If your marriage is in a challenging place, *The Marriage Experience* can definitely move you forward—but it is no substitute for professional help. You are actively seeking answers, a very hopeful pursuit. Be encouraged! But, it still may be necessary to make the call for help today. You can do this!

Wherever you are in your marriage, we are excited to be a part of this experience. God has given us so much grace in preparing this for you. We believe he has given you grace as well to connect with your spouse on a deeper level.

WHAT TO EXPECT

WHILE WE DON'T WANT you to feel like you have to follow a bunch of rules, we do believe that there are ways to go about your experience that will deeply enhance your time spent together. Read the guide below to prepare yourselves. Please do not skip this part. This is where your experience begins.

Each week begins with a prompt to prepare yourselves for your time together. Clear your mind of anything that is weighing you down: burdens, to-do lists, grievances, or even expectations of how this time together will go. Prepare your hearts for each other, for the here and now; this is not the time to work through major conflicts. Turn off all distractions, including phones, televisions, and other devices.

One crucial element to this experience is connection through questions. After the moment of preparation, there will be questions to ask each other. Don't skip this part! This isn't the time to rip open old wounds, but rather to discuss the previous week and plan for the week ahead of you. This light opening conversation will help you relax and focus on the instruction that follows.

After your opening conversation, you will find a short read covering the topic of the week, sharing relevant Bible references, practical stories, and application. The voice each week alternates between Ryan and Jenny, providing insights and perspective from both husband and wife on these foundational topics. You may want to take turns reading aloud.

During your conversation following the reading, be attentive to each other. Be vulnerable. Be expectant! You have a wonderful opportunity to learn more about your spouse and what God says about your relationship. Listen with an open mind when your spouse is speaking. Battle through discomfort, making room in your heart for change and improvement. Give this conversation as much time as it needs.

After you are finished, we strongly suggest praying with and for each other, either aloud or silently, together. (We encourage you to pray aloud eventually, but it's all right if you aren't comfortable in the beginning.) We like to take turns praying aloud from week to week. Try it!

MAXIMIZE YOUR MARRIAGE EXPERIENCE

THIS MAY BE THE first time you are setting aside intentional weekly conversation time with your spouse, or you may have tried in the past but not had a positive or pleasant experience. If so, here are a few suggestions that will help you enjoy a wonderful experience together:

Stay the course. Some weekly conversations will feel hard. We encourage you to have those tough talks with a gentle and loving spirit. Connecting through mind, body, and soul may not come naturally at first. Therefore, we have created an experience you can build on as your comfort level and connection grows. Stay with it.

Give it time. This time should be planned, prioritized, anticipated, and unhurried. Write it down in your shared calendar, and gently remind each other—let each other know you are looking forward to it. If possible, find a consistent time in your week to meet. Allow this experience to become a regular rhythm of communication for you. Don't allow others to steal this time from you and your spouse.

Eliminate distraction. Again, turn off or mute electronics. If you have other family members in the home, take care of their needs ahead of time, or meet after their bedtime. Your time together should not feel like an obligation, but rather a joint effort toward a unified goal. Be intentional about it, and enjoy your time.

Enhance your ability to connect by using all of your senses. Always find or create a comfortable environment. If your living room is cluttered or if toys are scattered everywhere, choose another room, or straighten up before your time together. The less your mind has to compete with, the more present you can be with your spouse. If you want to take this experience to the next level, add the following sensory elements:

- *Add an element of sound.* No, we're not talking about ocean waves or a classical melody, unless background sounds help you focus. Listen to the sound of *each other's voice*. Each week the reading alternates perspective. Amp up your experience: take turns reading aloud and guiding the action steps that follow.

- *Add an element of taste*. Experience your time together over a meal, cup of coffee or tea, or dessert. You don't have to do this every time; choose what's best for you. We often connect over coffee, and it truly adds a delightful element to our time together.
- *Incorporate smell into the experience*. Light a candle in the room or diffuse some oils. Take turns choosing the scent you prefer. It's ok if your spouse forgets or simply doesn't respond to this element. However, you should at least ensure there aren't any unpleasant smells in your space!

Let's begin.

PART ONE//FOUNDATIONS

||||||||||

SOME OF THE WORST examples of senseless loss of life come down to someone who forgot the basics, cut corners, or failed to maintain the integrity of the overall foundation. A battery is left unchanged and a house burns to the ground. A wound isn't cleaned properly, becomes infected, and a patient dies. A crack is ignored and a bridge collapses.

Strong foundations—and taking care of the basics—can be the difference between life and death. In marriage, your foundation, and those basic assumptions we often come to take for granted, can mean the difference between a marriage that struggles to survive and a marriage that is fulfilling beyond all imagination. In Part One//Foundations, each week we will look at a foundational aspect of marriage—and talk about it! As you begin *The Marriage Experience*, no matter where you are on your marriage journey, use these first thirteen weeks to make some course corrections: treat the unhealthy wounds so they don't fester; fix those cracks before they threaten your relationship; and recharge your batteries.

Make each week's time a priority; deflect interruptions. If you are unable to complete a week, do not skip it. Pick up where you left off as soon as you are able. It's time to check your foundation.

Let's start the conversation—Part One!

Ryan and Jenny

WEEK 1

||||||||||

CONNECTION

BEFORE YOU BEGIN

Take time to prepare your mind, your heart, and your space.
Be open to change; listen well and anticipate a positive experience.

START THE CONVERSATION

- What encouraged you this past week?
- What discouraged you this past week?
- What one thing can I do to help you in the week ahead?
- What are your prayer needs for the week ahead?

5-MINUTE READ-ALOUD

Jenny:

"I just don't feel connected to my spouse right now." Have you ever spoken or thought those words? If so, you are in good company. (I can say that because I am part of that company!) Connection is not going to happen accidentally. It requires effort. Connection takes energy and time, both of which are limited resources. Also, the ways in which we connect as a couple change over time, causing many couples to find themselves in a disconnected rut if they don't learn how to readjust, to "change with the tide." Ryan and I are certainly no exception. Just in the first fifteen years of our marriage, we had two children, lived in three cities, earned four degrees, and held seven jobs. It has been full, to say the least. Quite a few times over the years, we have found ourselves *dis*connected, and had to *re*connect by communicating with each other better and reprioritizing our relationship.

Connection is more than communication. Connection is more than sharing schedules and space together. Connection can and should happen on a spiritual, physical, and intellectual level. God has given us our spouse to love, respect, and enjoy! Without connection, we miss out on the fulfilling marriage he has in store for us.

Connection is more than communication.

Spiritually—God has called us into a relationship with him, first and foremost. When you and your spouse have a strong connection with the Lord and understand his love for you, then it will overflow into a spiritually connected relationship with each other. First John 4:19 says, "We love because he first loved us." You can connect spiritually by praying together, sharing your spiritual struggles or questions, or listening to and discussing a sermon or Bible study together.

Physically—God designed the act of sex as a *gift* for us within the confines of our marriage, but physical connection does not start, or end, with sex. Daily hugs, kisses, and being physically near to your spouse will communicate to them that you desire to be connected. Don't forget the small stuff! If your physical connection is lacking, it could be from unspoken needs or unrealistic expectations.

Intellectually—No one has ever accused me of being an intellectual (just being honest here), but Ryan and I have still found ways to connect through discussion of big ideas. Whether I ask him a theological question or we are reading a book together, having deep discussion has greatly increased our intellectual connection with each other.

How you connect with your spouse may change from season to season in your marriage. The important part is that you are *intentional* about it; communicate to your spouse that you *want* to connect, and then do it! Show them your desire for closeness with a text, being physically near them, asking them questions, and listening to them. Little acts of kindness go a long way (think "note on the mirror" or making them coffee). Show gratitude for their presence in your life; disconnect from electronics to prioritize personal time above anything else vying for your attention. Spend time together reminiscing, worshiping, seeking to understand each other's perspective, discussing deep thoughts, or doing an activity.

DIG DEEPER

Talk about it:

- We talked about the importance of spiritual, physical, and intellectual connection with your spouse. In which of these areas do you feel your connection is lacking in this season of your marriage?

Do it:

- How can you show your spouse today or tomorrow (or both) that your desire for closeness is a priority in your marriage?
- Choose one way to connect with your spouse this week. Make a note somewhere or set an alarm to remind you to connect in the way you have chosen.

PRAY FOR AND WITH EACH OTHER

WEEK 2

||||||||||

UNITY

BEFORE YOU BEGIN

Take time to prepare your mind, your heart, and your space.
Be open to change; listen well and anticipate a positive experience.

START THE CONVERSATION

- What encouraged you this past week?
- What discouraged you this past week?
- What one thing can I do to help you in the week ahead?
- What are your prayer needs for the week ahead?

5-MINUTE READ-ALOUD

Ryan:

Throughout the first two chapters of the Bible, we see that God creates many things, and it is good. Shortly after we read that God created Adam, Genesis 2:18 has the first mention of something that is "not good." God said that Adam needed a helper, and he created Eve from Adam. As we get to the end of the chapter, we see that Adam and Eve become one flesh as husband and wife—talk about being united together!

Often we will read this passage and misremember its foundational truth about marriage: the importance of *unity* in marital relationships.

On our wedding day, Jenny and I lit a unity candle, but at the time, I don't think we truly understood the significance of that part of the ceremony. In Matthew 19, Jesus spoke on the subject of marriage and divorce, and he quoted the passage from Genesis 2 on how a husband and wife are united as one flesh. He then went on to say in verse 6 that what God has joined together, "let not man separate."

How unified is your marriage?

The apostle Paul covered many subjects in the letters he wrote in the New Testament. Of all the topics he addressed, I would suggest that a call for unity is one of the most consistent. From I Corinthians to the book of Ephesians, he described unity in the church as vital in order for the church to accomplish the mission of making disciples among the nations.

The same is true for our marriages. Your ability to root out division in your marriage, and your insistence on unity within your marriage, will allow God to work in your marriage to grow your relationship to its fullest potential. It is not only in the church where God moves the mission, but also within the home.

> **Your ability to root out division in your marriage, and your insistence on unity within your marriage, will allow God to work in your marriage to grow your relationship to its fullest potential.**

Again, I ask, how unified is your marriage?

DIG DEEPER

Talk about it:
- In what areas in your marriage do you need unity? List five areas where unity is essential in any marriage relationship, then share your lists with each other.
- Together, choose two areas where you can grow in unity in *your* relationship.

PRAY FOR AND WITH EACH OTHER

WEEK 3

||||||||||

FORGIVENESS

BEFORE YOU BEGIN
Take time to prepare your mind, your heart, and your space.
Be open to change; listen well and anticipate a positive experience.

START THE CONVERSATION

- What encouraged you this past week?
- What discouraged you this past week?
- What one thing can I do to help you in the week ahead?
- What are your prayer needs for the week ahead?

5-MINUTE READ-ALOUD

Jenny:

So many parts of our marriage are awesome, amazing, and full of joy. However, our marriage is by no means perfect! Naturally, we are selfish human beings, and there is always room for improvement. With the need to improve comes the need to forgive. In a healthy marriage, we not only need to seek forgiveness, we need to be forgiving of each other as well. One is not necessarily mutually exclusive of the other. Often we need to forgive our partner, whether or not they acknowledge the issue, much less apologize and ask for *our* forgiveness. In Colossians 3:13, Paul told the church to "bear with each other," and this includes you and your spouse. While I would urge you to strive for a marriage that is much more than "bearing with" your spouse, there will be times it feels that way. Paul went on to say that if one has a complaint against another, "forgive as the Lord forgave you."

If you have a difficult time asking for forgiveness from your spouse, it may be because you did not see that model growing up.

One thing Ryan and I have tried to improve on over the years is seeking forgiveness as soon as we have offended the other, and offering forgiveness as soon as we have been offended. This has required a lot of humility, but it has served us well to acknowledge our imperfections *before* the offense festers and builds up, making forgiveness extremely challenging. It has also provided a healthy model to our kids, showing what forgiveness looks and sounds like in a marriage. If you have a difficult time asking for forgiveness from your spouse, it may be because you did not see that model growing up. Now is the best time to change that pattern for your own family.

I have heard it said that forgiveness is a gift you give yourself. Is there something your spouse has done in your past that you have not forgiven? Are you waiting for them to ask for your forgiveness? When you decide to forgive in your heart, you can begin to heal and move past it, clearing the way for a stronger marriage. Ask God to help you forgive your spouse, just as Christ has forgiven you.

DIG DEEPER

Talk about it:
- Without hashing through past hurts, talk to each other about what behaviors in general hurt your spirit. Sometimes it just takes a certain look or tone of voice, being judgmental, or forgetting something you agreed to.

Apply it:
- This week, your spouse may offend you. Try not to "fire back" in the heat of the moment. Find a time, hopefully before the day

is over, when both of you are calm. Lovingly help your spouse understand why you were offended.

- You may be the one who offends your spouse this week, perhaps without realizing it. If so, the moment you become aware of the offense, immediately and humbly seek forgiveness.

PRAY FOR AND WITH EACH OTHER

WEEK 4

||||||||||

HUMILITY

BEFORE YOU BEGIN

Take time to prepare your mind, your heart, and your space.
Be open to change; listen well and anticipate a positive experience.

START THE CONVERSATION

- What encouraged you this past week?
- What discouraged you this past week?
- What one thing can I do to help you in the week ahead?
- What are your prayer needs for the week ahead?

5-MINUTE READ-ALOUD

Ryan:

Do you like to road-trip or take long drives? When Jenny and I first began dating, the price of gas was low, and we would just drive around the city for hours. We would listen to some of our favorite CDs in the car and sing our hearts out! Interestingly, we were not as concerned about where we were going; sometimes when we thought we were getting close to a destination, we discovered that we were actually further away than ever—but it didn't matter to us. You see, we could never truly arrive at our destination, because the point was actually to be on the journey.

The same thing is true when it comes to humility. If you ever believe that you have "arrived" at a place of true humility, then in reality you are farther away. It's a journey.

Rick Warren said in his best-selling book, *The Purpose Driven Life,*[1] "Humility is not thinking less of yourself; it's thinking of yourself less." This means you realize that the world, and even your own life, does not revolve around you. This means you focus on God and others instead of yourself. Colossians 3:12 says, "Put on then, as God's chosen ones, holy and beloved, compassionate hearts, kindness, *humility*, meekness, and patience" (emphasis mine).

In your marriage, this means placing your spouse's needs above your own. This means serving your spouse. This means being others-focused. Read Colossians 3:12 again; while being humble is something believers should actively seek, in this verse we see that humility is, in reality, a gift we receive from God. Therefore, we *put on*, or *clothe* ourselves, in humility. Often, this can be a struggle for husbands. We want to be seen as confident, competent, and strong for our wives. Nevertheless, when we are weak, Jesus is strong.

> *Jenny*: Humility is an attitude that can take the form of both small and large acts. One particular time, Ryan demonstrated a very large act of humility in our marriage when we decided I should resign from my full-time job and stay at home with our second child. Two incomes made life financially comfortable, but at what cost to our family and to my own mental health? Ryan put my needs above his own when he chose to be the sole provider in our home, without putting any guilt or pressure on me.

Humility is a gift we receive from God.

Jesus did not come to earth thinking all about himself. He came thinking about you. He died for you and gave up his life for you. Put on the humility of Jesus!

DIG DEEPER

Do it:

How can you follow Jesus' example this week and humble yourself for the sake of your spouse? In other words, where can you put their needs before your own?

Talk about it:

Even if you have a thought about how to do this, ask your spouse what they need or want. They may have difficulty expressing this in words, so just look around. You may see something obvious. Then be sure to follow through with your commitment and talk about it next week.

PRAY FOR AND WITH EACH OTHER

WEEK 5

||||||||||

SUBMISSION

BEFORE YOU BEGIN

Take time to prepare your mind, your heart, and your space.
Be open to change; listen well and anticipate a positive experience.

START THE CONVERSATION

- What encouraged you this past week?
- What discouraged you this past week?
- What one thing can I do to help you in the week ahead?
- What are your prayer needs for the week ahead?

5-MINUTE READ-ALOUD

Jenny:

Oh, the "S" word, the word that a large part of our society would like you to believe is bad—that being *submissive* is harmful to your feminist views and modern ideology. Get that thought out of your head! Now listen up. God calls us to love *like him.* God calls us to obey him. God calls a husband and wife to "submit *to one another* out of reverence for Christ" (Ephesians 5:21, emphasis mine). Let me say that again. First, a husband and wife are to submit, or as Ryan refers to it, "fall under one mission," under God, as a sign of honor and deep respect for our Savior.

Submission: "falling under one mission."

Likewise, a wife is to fall under her husband's mission in the household as the spiritual leader. As a wife, I understand that this is a huge responsibility for my husband. I also understand that my husband is imperfect and does not always do, say, or think the things that Christ would want. However, my covenant with my spouse isn't conditional; I don't get to pick and choose when I submit and when I don't based upon my feelings toward his actions. I must submit to him out of respect for God and for my husband. I love how Lisa Chan puts it in the book *You and Me Forever: Marriage in Light of Eternity*[2]. She writes that submission is a respect for a "God-given position, and not perfection." She quotes Acts 5:29 to clarify that "only our submission to God should be absolute." However, please know that I am not suggesting your husband has the authority to force you into sin.

Submission is not easy, but that is no secret at this point. The reason you picked up this book is not that marriage is easy. Working toward a marriage that more closely resembles Christ is *hard*—but it's worth it. Chan notes that submitting to our husbands is our biblical calling, saying "there is no safer place to be than in the will of God." However, she also reminds us "the biblical concept of submission does not put your husband in the place of God." Submitting to our husbands is our way of showing them that we trust and support their godly leadership in our homes. It is not a license for abuse.

Husbands, please understand that many of us wives do not know how submission is supposed to look in our marriages. We are learning, as you are. Staying in safe communication (gentle, non-critical, regular) with each other will allow you to speak honest words to each other. Do you feel respected through your wife's submission? Are you honoring her thoughts and perspective as your God-given helper? If you are, it will be easier for her to submit to you, or "fall under your mission," knowing she has a role in God's mission for your family.

DIG DEEPER

Pray about it:
Wives, take time now to pray about it. Do you struggle to pray about submission, much less submit to your husband's leadership? Try this prayer:

"Dear Lord, help me to love like you and obey you, as your Word clearly states. Help me to submit first to you, and then give me the desire and design to submit to my husband, out of obedience to you and respect for him. Increase my desire to show him through submission that I trust and support his God-given leadership in our home. Amen."

PRAY FOR AND WITH EACH OTHER

WEEK 6

||||||||||

LEADERSHIP

BEFORE YOU BEGIN

Take time to prepare your mind, your heart, and your space.
Be open to change; listen well and anticipate a positive experience.

START THE CONVERSATION

- What encouraged you this past week?
- What discouraged you this past week?
- What one thing can I do to help you in the week ahead?
- What are your prayer needs for the week ahead?

5-MINUTE READ-ALOUD

Ryan:

In their book, *Designed to Lead*, authors Eric Geiger and Kevin Peck say, "Leadership is much like nuclear energy. It is able to warm a whole city or bring it to waste in death and destruction; it's all in how it is used."

This is certainly the case in a Christian marriage. The Bible is clear that the husband is to be the spiritual leader in the home. Is this the case in your marriage?

The Bible is clear that the husband is to be the spiritual leader in the home.

This idea, that the husband has headship in the home, is something that coincides perfectly with the call for the wife to submit to her husband (see Ephesians 5:22–33). Yet, so often, the husband's spiritual leadership in the home is nonexistent or abused, which leads to destruction.

Husbands, you are called to be the spiritual leader in your marriage—not from out front, dragging her along and demanding that she obediently go where you go, but also not from behind, following in her footsteps because you just want to "keep the peace." Rather, lead your wife from a place of humility. Stand next to her and take her hand. Communicate where you are going, and do so in a way that seeks after Jesus Christ and the path that he has set before you.

When our daughter was born, I wanted to establish a weekly time where we sang some worship songs, read the Bible, and prayed together as a family. To make a long story short, it took quite a bit of time—and humility—to make this a discipline in our home. While Jenny certainly was not against it, she did not make it a priority at first. One option would have been to give up, because it was not easy doing family worship with an infant. A second option could have been to force family worship, and I think you know how that would have gone. So, I tried to lead humbly (even though I sometimes failed along the way) and show the value I thought a regular family worship time would have on our family. Being an assertive and confident husband and leader in your marriage does not mean you are not able to lead in humility. In fact, I would say that they are two sides of the same coin when it comes to being a godly husband.

DIG DEEPER

Think about it:
Husbands, take a quick inventory, and ask yourself the following questions about your leadership within your marriage:

- Who in the marriage puts a greater emphasis on praying together?
- Who in the marriage is the driving force for going to church, even when you do not feel like going?
- How often do you ask your wife about spiritual things in the course of a week?

Do it:

Husbands, if your answers indicate that you are not the spiritual leader in your relationship, then choose one of these three areas (prayer, church, spiritual conversations) where you can take an intentional step toward spiritual leadership. Wives, encourage and pray for your husband as he seeks to fulfill his role as spiritual leader in your relationship.

PRAY FOR AND WITH EACH OTHER

WEEK 7

||||||||||

RESPECT

BEFORE YOU BEGIN

Take time to prepare your mind, your heart, and your space.
Be open to change; listen well and anticipate a positive experience.

START THE CONVERSATION

- What encouraged you this past week?
- What discouraged you this past week?
- What one thing can I do to help you in the week ahead?
- What are your prayer needs for the week ahead?

5-MINUTE READ-ALOUD

Jenny:

If you have read Dr. Emerson Eggerichs' book *Love and Respect*, then it will come as no surprise that I am writing on this topic, and for good reason. We could probably write an entire book on reasons and ways we love and respect our spouses! The Oxford Dictionary defines respect as "a feeling of admiration for someone or something because of their good qualities or achievements."[3] As respect goes, the age-old question remains: Which came first, the chicken or the egg? In your marriage, does respect foster deeper love, or does love foster deeper respect?

While I am not going to answer this question directly, I understand how society has skewed our vision of what respecting our husbands means. By Oxford's definition, respect should be the result of a demonstrated ability or quality. In reality, many women find it difficult to respect their husbands because they have not "earned it." Like it or not, the biblical concepts of respect and submission are deeply connected. In Ephesians 5:22, Paul did *not* tell wives to respect their husband "once they earned it," or *if* they earned it. He said, "Wives, submit yourselves to your own husbands as you do to the Lord." Paul was saying that, in order to have a God-honoring marriage, you *must* respect your husband's God-given authority over the marriage. It's not up to your discretion to respect your husband only if he has earned it. And, having a God-honoring marriage should be our goal as a couple.

It's not up to your discretion to respect your husband only if he has earned it.

Respect and submission are connected—two sides to the same coin, as Ryan would say. Respect is an attitude of the heart; submission is an expression of that attitude. Wives are given a biblical call to *respect* their husband's God-given leadership role; therefore, wives should *submit* to their leadership as a loving expression of our respect for our husbands.

Wives, you can respect your husband's authority in many ways. For example, consult him when making decisions for the family, even the small ones. I once heard a husband say that he may not even care one way or the other all the time, but he at least wants to be asked.

Respect means encouraging the person he *is*—not the one you *want* him to be (or hoped he would become once you were married). Wives, your husband will feel respected when you point out his attributes and strengths rather than his faults and weaknesses; give him grace when, not *if*, he fails.

Respecting your husband shows him you trust his guidance and authority and that you believe in his ability to lead your family the way that God intended.

DIG DEEPER

Talk about it:
- Wives, name one or two strengths that you see in your husband's leadership. Thank him for what he does well to lead your family.
- Are there areas you have controlled the decision-making process in your marriage where you can allow him in (kids, activities, meals, vacations, holidays)?
- Are there some major areas you want and need his leadership in, like budget or discipline? Name one and ask your husband to weigh in. Remember, this is a safe place to talk about important things!

PRAY FOR AND WITH EACH OTHER

WEEK 8

||||||||||

ACCOUNTABILITY

BEFORE YOU BEGIN

Take time to prepare your mind, your heart, and your space.
Be open to change; listen well and anticipate a positive experience.

START THE CONVERSATION

- What encouraged you this past week?
- What discouraged you this past week?
- What one thing can I do to help you in the week ahead?
- What are your prayer needs for the week ahead?

5-MINUTE READ-ALOUD

Ryan:

Keeping someone accountable is not easy. Letting someone keep you accountable is even harder. In his book *The Advantage*, leadership guru Patrick Lencioni writes this about accountability:

> Many leaders who struggle with accountability try to convince themselves that their reluctance is a product of their kindness; they just don't want to make employees feel bad. But an honest assessment of their motivation will allow them to admit that they are the ones who don't want to feel bad and that failing to hold someone accountable is ultimately an act of selfishness.

This same concept applies to our marriages. We are responsible for helping each other live godly lives by keeping each other accountable. Men, how often do you fail to have hard conversations with your wife, telling yourself you do not want to hurt her feelings? Wives, when you decide *not* to speak up to address an issue with your husband, do you tell yourself you are protecting his self-esteem?

What we are really doing is avoiding conflict, and our motives are selfish. In Ephesians 4 Paul spoke about the building up of the church in unity through the work of its members. We go on to read that believers should speak the truth in love; from these difficult conversations, we grow to look more like Jesus.

Speaking the truth in love is hard, but so important. Truth without love is judgmental and condescending. Love without truth is nothing more than tolerance, and does not lead to growth. Speaking love and truth to your spouse keeps you both accountable.

While it is great to also have an accountability partner or group of the same gender, your spouse should be your "go-to" with your burdens, and with your transgressions. In James 5:16 we are told to confess our sins to each other and to pray for one another. Do you regularly communicate your struggles with your spouse so that they can hold you accountable? When your spouse shares their issues, how do you receive them? Do you quickly dismiss their admissions? Do you respond with a critical spirit, or are you tender and compassionate?

How are you keeping each other accountable? You and your spouse are constantly changing. Therefore, your relationship is changing as well. Change without accountability leads to pain. Change *with* accountability leads to progress.

Change with accountability leads to progress.

DIG DEEPER

Talk about it:
Take some time to answer the following questions with your spouse:

- Do you regularly communicate your struggles with your spouse? If not, take time now.
- When you listen to your spouse's issue, how do you receive it? Does your spouse feel loved by your response, even if the issue is hard for you to hear?
- How are you keeping each other accountable? Is there a way to be proactive rather than waiting until one of you fails in some way?

PRAY FOR AND WITH EACH OTHER

WEEK 9

||||||||||

INFLUENCE

BEFORE YOU BEGIN

Take time to prepare your mind, your heart, and your space.
Be open to change; listen well and anticipate a positive experience.

START THE CONVERSATION

- What encouraged you this past week?
- What discouraged you this past week?
- What one thing can I do to help you in the week ahead?
- What are your prayer needs for the week ahead?

5-MINUTE READ-ALOUD

Jenny:

Because of social media, the word *influence* has a different connotation to me now than it would have had ten years ago. We are very aware of social media influencers telling us what we should buy, how a "perfect" home should look, and so on. Still, the idea of influence has been around since the creation of the world. Enter, the serpent in the garden, right? Satan's influence led Eve to go for that forbidden fruit.

Did you know your marriage has a huge influence on others?

Throughout the New Testament, we are prompted to act like Christ, and much of what the apostle Paul wrote was to encourage the leaders of the church, and the church itself, to live in a manner worthy of Christ so as not to lose our testimony. In Titus 2:7-8, Paul prompted Titus to teach the believers under his leadership to act in such a way that those who were opposed to their beliefs could not condemn them. The same holds true for how we act today, especially in our marriages. If we proclaim to be Christians, people naturally look to us to provide an influence in their lives. It's up to us to make sure our influence points them to Christ. That is a heavy responsibility, and it does not mean we should never let others see our struggles. Being vulnerable with a few people and sharing your struggles can still point people to Christ. Alisha Illian wrote in *Chasing Perfect*[4] "our flaws and failures don't keep us from Christ—they draw us to Him." She goes on to advise us, "Be authentic with all, transparent with some, and vulnerable with a few."

How is the secular world influencing your marriage?

Many people did not grow up with a model of what a healthy Christian marriage looks like. Unfortunately, many people who lack this healthy model find a different influence in unhealthy places. Secular media glamorizes affairs, multiple partners, and cohabitation. We glorify celebrity marriages (even Christian celebrities), then are deeply hurt and even troubled when they come crashing down off that pedestal we put them on.

Consider this: what people see in your marriage might have a great influence on their own marriage. Additionally, your relationship with your spouse could, ideally, point others to Jesus. This truth is one of the main reasons we created this experience for you. Take a moment and reflect on our introduction again. We said:

> Did you know that your marriage has a purpose beyond your own personal fulfillment and companionship, as important as that is?. . . A healthy, happy marriage not only brings lasting love and fulfillment to you and your family but also strengthens your understanding of God. Beyond that, your marriage, both in sacrifice and in strength, puts on display the relationship between Jesus and his bride, the church.

Your marriage is part of God's design to reach the lost. How can we positively influence other marriages around us? This does not mean "all access" to all of our issues, but neither does it mean we should only show the highlight reel. Do you sometimes speak disrespectfully or unlovingly about your spouse with your coworkers, casual friends, or family members? In public, we need to make sure we are lifting our spouses up and only speaking well of them. Be honest and vulnerable with those you have relational equity and trust with—do not pretend you are doing well when you need accountability.

Your marriage is part of God's design to reach the lost.

DIG DEEPER

Talk about it:
- What steps can you take this week to improve the marital influence you have on the world around you? Together, choose one action to do this week, and then hold each other to it.

Do it:
- What steps can you take this week to reduce or remove the negative influence the world has on your marriage? This action step can be hard; it may require you break off a relationship or agree not to participate in certain unhealthy activities (i.e., social media, unhealthy television shows, or movies).

- **Bonus:** Social media influence isn't all bad! Shout out to your spouse on social media or especially when talking with your kids or friends. Sharing your love and encouragement publicly helps your connection with your spouse too! Just be sure you are being authentic and that your desire is to lift up your spouse, not public recognition or to put up a false image. And remember – public praise is no substitute for consistent, private encouragement.

PRAY FOR AND WITH EACH OTHER

WEEK 10

||||||||||

COMMUNITY

BEFORE YOU BEGIN

Take time to prepare your mind, your heart, and your space.
Be open to change; listen well and anticipate a positive experience.

START THE CONVERSATION

- What encouraged you this past week?
- What discouraged you this past week?
- What one thing can I do to help you in the week ahead?
- What are your prayer needs for the week ahead?

5-MINUTE READ-ALOUD

Ryan:

On Week 2, I spoke about unity in our marriage relationships, and I directed you to the book of Genesis. I would like to turn your attention there again today. In the first chapter of Genesis, as we read the creation account, we repeatedly see the phrase "it was good" (1:10, 12, 18, 21, and 25). Not until Genesis 2:18 do we read something was *not* good. It is there we see that it was not good for man to be alone.

God intended for man to be in community from the beginning. In Genesis 1:26, we read that God said, "Let us create man in our image, after our likeness." The Trinity (God the Father, God the Son, and God the Holy Spirit) has existed since eternity past, and they have lived in community.

Now, here is the *really* cool part: the marriage relationship between man and woman is the cornerstone of the model for community God built for humanity. The relationship you have with your spouse should be your first priority for community. So, what does this look like in your marriage? How are you intentionally taking time to invest in your wife? How are you spending your relational energy on your husband?

It is only after you have this healthy kind of community with your spouse that you can have community with others around you. If you do not have healthy community with your spouse, then you will seek to fill this void with others—and this will lead down a devastating path.

> **If you do not have healthy community with your spouse, then you will seek to fill this void with others— and this will lead down a devastating path.**

With that said, it is crucial to have community as a married couple with other married couples. Seek peer relationships with other couples. Seek relationships with mentor couples that are more spiritually mature than you are. Finally, seek community with younger couples that need mentoring. These relationships build a healthy Christian community that will produce joy, love, growth, accountability, and discipleship.

How might you seek to enter into deeper community with your spouse this week?

DIG DEEPER

Talk about it:
As a couple, you should seek community in relationships with other couples. Take some time to evaluate if you have community in the following ways:

- Do you have a relationship with at least one mentor couple that is more spiritually mature? If not, can you think of two or three couples who might fill this void?
- Do you have community with at least one younger couple that

needs mentoring? If not, can you think of two or three couples whom you might be able to build a relationship with?

- Do you have peer relationships with other couples where you are doing life together?

Do it:
Make a commitment to spend time with at least one of these couples in the next few weeks. Call them and get it on your calendar in the next few days.

PRAY FOR AND WITH EACH OTHER

WEEK 11

||||||||||

ENCOURAGEMENT

BEFORE YOU BEGIN

Take time to prepare your mind, your heart, and your space.
Be open to change; listen well and anticipate a positive experience.

START THE CONVERSATION

- What encouraged you this past week?
- What discouraged you this past week?
- What one thing can I do to help you in the week ahead?
- What are your prayer needs for the week ahead?

5-MINUTE READ-ALOUD

Jenny:

"I believe in you. You can do this. You have what it takes." What encouraging messages! Encouragement means to inspire courage, to push someone forward in their pursuits. Have you ever heard such a message directed toward you, maybe from a parent, teacher, coach, or friend? Have you ever heard it from your spouse? Or rather, have you ever spoken these words of encouragement *to* your spouse? Let that sink in for a moment. When was the last time you encouraged your spouse?

If you cannot remember the last time you encouraged your spouse, let me challenge you to do so with words *and* action. Many times, encouragement can be the difference between success and failure in your pursuits, particularly if it comes from your spouse.

Encouragement can be the difference between success and failure in your pursuits, particularly if it comes from your spouse.

After we had been married about five years, I decided to go to graduate school. Ryan encouraged me verbally with great confidence and support, and it made *all* the difference. However, as mentioned before, encouragement takes words *and* action. We cannot just *say* we believe in our spouse when our *actions* don't agree. I did a lot of my schoolwork on the weekend instead of spending time with Ryan. Among other things, he demonstrated his encouragement by taking over some of my responsibilities and giving me the space I needed. When Ryan received God's call to leave his steadily rising bank career and go into the ministry, it meant sacrificing our comfortable life and financially promising future. It required going to seminary. We discussed it together and I submitted to his authority, but also was 100 percent on board with this dramatic change. We sold our home, moved away from our friends and church home, and lived with his parents for a year. I cannot imagine where our marriage would be today if I had grumbled and complained or, worse yet, refused to move. An unsupportive and discouraging spouse can easily derail us from God's best in our lives.

Do you know what challenge your spouse is facing right now? If not, start by simply asking. Then show your support by speaking truth to them and following up with action. Do not assume they already know you support them. Try sending them a text or leaving a message on the bathroom mirror. Your encouraging action might mean a sacrifice of habit or routine, time, energy, and even money, or something you have wanted. We believe in you and your marriage, and we sacrificed a lot to bring *you* a word of encouragement. You can do this. You have what it takes to have a loving, encouraging, life-giving marriage.

DIG DEEPER

Talk about it:

- Tell each other one of your greatest challenges at work or at home, or talk about an unfulfilled dream or goal.
- Take turns encouraging each other in those specific challenges. Make a note to tell them again later in the week (or even daily, if words of affirmation are their love language).
- Talk about one thing you can do for each other that will alleviate some obstacles or move each of you forward. Then, schedule it. Take responsibility and follow up your encouraging words with action!

PRAY FOR AND WITH EACH OTHER

WEEK 12

||||||||||

DISCIPLINE

Take time to prepare your mind, your heart, and your space.
Be open to change; listen well and anticipate a positive experience.

START THE CONVERSATION

- What encouraged you this past week?
- What discouraged you this past week?
- What one thing can I do to help you in the week ahead?
- What are your prayer needs for the week ahead?

5-MINUTE READ-ALOUD

Ryan:

Have you heard of *Jeet Kune Do*? No? Well, you are not alone. *Jeet Kune Do* is a hybrid form of martial arts that originated in 1967. While you may not be familiar with this kind of discipline, you may have heard of its creator—Bruce Lee.

Known as "the way of the intercepting fist," this martial arts discipline was founded on the principle of attacking an opponent at the moment he is about to attack. Lee's goal was to remove the limitations found in any one fighting form so that one could have the freedom to "be like water" and adapt to each situation. And, like most disciplines, mastering this style of fighting takes a great deal of patience and practice. In other words, it would take a lot of pain at the beginning to bring freedom in the end.

The Bible has a lot to say about discipline. One of my favorite passages is found in Hebrews 12:5–11. The final two verses say this:

> For they disciplined us for a short time as it seemed best to them, but he disciplines us for our good, that we may share his holiness. For the moment all discipline seems painful rather than pleasant, but later it yields the peaceful fruit of righteousness to those who have been trained by it.

Throughout the book of Hebrews, the author encouraged his readers to stay faithful, to look to the future with hope, and to sacrifice the things of man for the things of God. Here in this passage, we see a discourse on discipline, and it certainly can be applied to marriage.

While it seems easy to live in a land of flowers and bubbles when you first get married (Jenny, our marriage is still flowers and bubbles), it doesn't take long before the honeymoon is over. However, if both the husband and the wife practice discipline in their marriage, in the way they live, in how they love each other, then some temporary pain will create lasting joy.

Most of us are disciplined in some area of our lives; we work out regularly, show up to work on time, and would never miss our favorite sporting events, yet we have no such disciplines in the context of our marriages.

Discipline in your marriage brings freedom.

Look at each of the topics we have discussed in *The Marriage Experience*: connection, unity, forgiveness, humility, submission, leadership, respect, accountability, influence, community, and encouragement. Each one is both a characteristic of a healthy marriage and a *discipline*. Each one requires you to take intentional steps to build that discipline into your life.

For our marriage discipline of *connection*, we set aside weekly, uninterrupted time to talk about our marriage (hopefully something similar to what you are doing right now as you go through this book). At first, this discipline had some pain points as we talked about important yet difficult issues in our marriage. However, having been consistent in this discipline, we have found freedom and growth in our relationship. Perhaps you felt some of these painful or difficult moments as you went through *The Marriage Experience*. If so, stay the course. A little pain now will bring freedom in the end.

DIG DEEPER

Talk about it:
- Review the list of marriage disciplines above. Each of you individually write down what you think your strongest and weakest marriage disciplines are right now.
- Compare your lists and talk about the differences. Where are your marriage instabilities, and what disciplines might you practice to strengthen those areas?
- Have you set aside weekly time or made intentional effort to build any of these disciplines into your marriage experience? If so, what is going well and what could you improve? If not, what step will you take in order to establish that discipline?

PRAY FOR AND WITH EACH OTHER

WEEK 13

||||||||||

CELEBRATION

BEFORE YOU BEGIN

Take time to prepare your mind, your heart, and your space.
Be open to change; listen well and anticipate a positive experience.

START THE CONVERSATION

- What encouraged you this past week?
- What discouraged you this past week?
- What one thing can I do to help you in the week ahead?
- What are your prayer needs for the week ahead?

5 -MINUTE READ-ALOUD

You did it! Whether or not this was your first time studying together, praying together, or spending a consistent amount of intentional time together, we are proud of you! Your experience may not have been what you expected; some weeks were probably more difficult than others. Marriage can be hard. Choosing each other can be hard. You were meant to do hard things, and you did! You are now finished with Part One// Foundations! As with any project or completed task, we encourage you to celebrate a job well done. We have outlined a few ideas below to give you a kick-start.

You were meant to do hard things.

Reflect on it: Each of you, sum up your thoughts about the experience in a few words or phrases, and write it down where you can see it. If you journal, then journal it. If you write on sticky notes, then write it there. If you keep things in your calendar, that's great also! Encourage each other in what you just accomplished together by sharing your thoughts.

Share it: Share the love with another couple who you think could benefit by gifting them this experience. Perhaps you know a couple who is newly married or engaged. What a great gift this would be to start them out on their marital journey!

Do it: Do you have an activity you have wanted to do together, but never had a reason? This is your sign. Sign up for that class, throw that ax, escape that room, take that trip, make that meal—you get the idea.

Show it: Show the world, or at least your community, that you are on fire for God and each other. Continue to put Jesus on display through your marriage. Seeing your love on display will spark an interest in someone else that could lead to gospel conversations.

Write it: Write each other a letter sharing your gratitude for their interest in your marriage. Ryan and I keep journals designed to leave love notes for each other (it also saves a ton of money in the greeting card department). That would be a great place for encouragement and continued affection.

Dream it: Take a moment and dream together. Look how far you have come, and talk about where you want your marriage to go next.

Give it: Give your loved one a little token of your affection. It does not have to be a big gesture or cost a lot of money. Let it be a reminder of this shared experience.

Continue it: Read the intro to the next unit and hit the gas!

PRAY FOR AND WITH EACH OTHER

PART TWO//FRUIT

||||||||||

DID YOU KNOW THERE is a strong connection between the marriage relationship and the Holy Spirit? In Part Two//Fruit, each week we will look at an aspect of the fruit of the Spirit, a wonderful description of what it looks like when we are allowing the Holy Spirit to be in control, found in Galatians 5:22–23. In the context of our marriages, this perspective is refreshing and eye opening! As you go deeper into *The Marriage Experience*, your journey may get a little tougher, conversations a little deeper. This is all part of the design. Keep going! The exhilarating reward at the end will be well worth it.

In Part One, you may remember that your marriage has a purpose beyond your own personal fulfillment and companionship. Part Two includes many steps to help you fulfill that purpose as you grow closer and closer together and learn to *experience* the fruits of your marriage. Just like Part One, we designed this series in a twelve-week unit, closing with suggestions for an enjoyable celebration activity. Make each week's time a priority; deflect interruptions. If you are unable to complete a week, do not skip it. Pick up where you left off as soon as you are able.

Let's start the conversation—Part Two!

Ryan and Jenny

WEEK 1

||||||||

LOVE

But the fruit of the Spirit is ***love,*** joy, peace, patience,
kindness, goodness, faithfulness, gentleness, self-control;
against such things there is no law.
GALATIANS 5:22–23 ESV

BEFORE YOU BEGIN
Take time to prepare your mind, your heart, and your space.
Be open to change; listen well and anticipate a positive experience.

START THE CONVERSATION
- What encouraged you this past week?
- What discouraged you this past week?
- What one thing can I do to help you in the week ahead?
- What are your prayer needs for the week ahead?

5-MINUTE READ-ALOUD
Ryan:
The Beatles famously sang, "Love is all you need.[5]" Do you think that this
is true?

I would say yes… or maybe no. It really depends on what you mean
by *love.*

In our twenty-first century American culture, most people function-
ally view love as something you feel. If it makes you feel good, then you

might classify it as love. If it helps you deal with things, then it's love. If it helps you discover the "real" you, then it must be love.

But I would suggest something different. The Bible would say that love is *so* much more than a feeling, a temporary fix for our problems, or how we find worth in ourselves.

In 1 John 4:7–11, we read this:

> Beloved, let us love one another, for love is from God, and whoever loves has been born of God and knows God. Anyone who does not love does not know God, because God is love. In this the love of God was made manifest among us, that God sent his only Son into the world, so that we might live through him. In this is love, not that we have loved God but that he loved us and sent his Son to be the propitiation for our sins. Beloved, if God so loved us, we also ought to love one another.

Did you catch that? *God* is love. Let me say it again, *God is love.*

If this is true, then the first fruit of the Spirit in your life and in your marriage is *love.* To put it a different way, your love for each other reflects God himself to an empty and confused world. And this love (which is God) is shown to us through God sending his Son, Jesus, into the world. Remember John 3:16? This is the first verse most young children learn in church: "For God so loved the world that he gave his only Son, that whoever believes in him should not perish but have eternal life."

Your love for each other reflects God himself to an empty and confused world.

In Part One of *The Marriage Experience*, we discussed the truth that your marriage is meant for so much more than feeling good or making your spouse feel good. A vibrant, healthy marriage goes beyond personal fulfillment and companionship. The purpose of marriage is to put the relationship between Jesus and the church on display. When you do this, you show the world the love of God. Your marriage will magnify the love of Jesus. Your marriage will put the gospel on display.

With this understanding, we must believe that love is more than feeling. We see that love is action. We see that love is sacrifice. We see that love is meant to be a reflection of God to the world, manifested through our marriage. Don't worry if you struggle to understand this or are concerned your marriage does not do this. Next week Jenny will go deeper into this verse and this idea of what God's love looks like in a marriage.

For now, I want you to think about love as an action in the context of your marriage.

DIG DEEPER

Think about it:

- Did the love in your marriage begin primarily as a feeling? How has this view evolved since you were first married?
- How has your love for your spouse shown up in action this past week? Were there times when you may have been unloving?
- In what ways have you put God's love (God) on display in your marriage? In other words, in what ways does your marriage reflect the gospel (the love of Jesus) to the world?
- Did you struggle to answer the last question? Perhaps you did not like the answer. If so, next week Jenny will give you some helpful insights into how to do this.

PRAY FOR AND WITH EACH OTHER

WEEK 2

|||||||||

MORE LOVE

But the fruit of the Spirit is **love,** joy, peace, patience,
kindness, goodness, faithfulness, gentleness, self-control;
against such things there is no law.
GALATIANS 5:22–23 ESV

BEFORE YOU BEGIN
Take time to prepare your mind, your heart, and your space.
Be open to change; listen well and anticipate a positive experience.

START THE CONVERSATION
- What encouraged you this past week?
- What discouraged you this past week?
- What one thing can I do to help you in the week ahead?
- What are your prayer needs for the week ahead?

5-MINUTE READ-ALOUD
Jenny:

Love is such a broad topic, and one on which entire books have been
written. Big books. Heavy books. To condense it to just a couple pages
hardly seems possible. Where do I even begin? How about the source?
Ryan just introduced you to the definition of love found in 1 John 4:7–11.
Verse 8 tells us God himself is love. Let's unpack what this means and
what it has to do with our love with our spouse. God is love incarnate,
or love in bodily form. He is the One to whom all other definitions of

love should be compared. He shows us sacrificial love, undeserved and unconditional love. To know God's love is to know *how* to love. The best way to know God's love is to read in the Bible how Jesus loved others.

You cannot love like a God you don't truly know, so let's start there. Let's start with an unbroken, loving fellowship with our Savior. The more you come to know and experience God's love on a personal, intimate level, the more that love will overflow into your relationships with others, including—and especially—your spouse.

To know God's love is to know how to love.

Love, like all of the other spiritual fruit found in Galatians 5:22–23 (joy, peace, patience, kindness, goodness, faithfulness, gentleness, and self-control), is not always easy. Sure, when our spouses agree with us or act in accordance with what we desire, loving them is easy. But what about when our spouses act selfishly? What about when we don't get our way? Loving our spouses the way God loves us can become extremely challenging. Let's think of the example we have in God, who created us in his image to be love on earth. We mess this up daily, hourly perhaps, yet he still loves us.

Do you feel like your spouse pesters you? Nags? Demands their own way? Now think about your attitude toward God when you come to him in prayer. Do you ever make demands of God? Do you ever express your frustration to God? I know I do. Yet, he still loves you. Does your spouse seem selfish or self-serving in how they spend their time, or in a lack of desire to do things for you? That pretty much sums up how I mess up with God on a regular basis when he calls me to do something I do not want to do. Yet, he still loves me.

Remember, 1 John 4:8 tells us that God is love, but what does that look like? Let's review a familiar verse:

> Love is patient and kind; love does not envy or boast; it is not arrogant or rude. It does not insist on its own way; it is not irritable or resentful; it does not rejoice at wrongdoing, but rejoices with the truth. Love bears all things, believes all things, hopes all things, endures all things. Love never ends. (1 Corinthians 13:4–8 ESV)

Want to see how you are doing in the "love" department? Try substituting your name for "love" in the above passage and see if it rings true. "Jenny is patient and kind; Jenny does not envy or boast; she is not arrogant or rude..." How does that sit with your heart? Paul was speaking to the church here, not to couples specifically. However, it's worth noting that his emphasis was our underlying motive—love. We should live in a way where love is the foundation of everything we say and do.

This passage in 1 Corinthians 13 is all action. It describes how God loves us, and gives us a roadmap on how we should ask his Holy Spirit to help us love our spouses. This supernatural love does not come easily. Don't put off loving the way God called you to love simply because it seems too difficult. Dream big and start small. Choose one way to love your spouse with this verse as your guide, and do it. Husbands, do you struggle to "bear all things" when it comes to your wife? Try asking the Lord specifically for loving patience toward her. Wives, do you tend to talk negatively to—or about—your husband? Ask the Lord for a self-controlled love (and stop talking negatively about your spouse!).

When we know and understand how undeserving we are of Christ's love, it puts into perspective the love that we are to show others, especially our spouses, the ones we are supposed to love most on this earth. We mess up. God promised to love us anyway. We promised the same for our spouses when we made our marriage covenant with them. Let's live out that love the way God intended.

DIG DEEPER

Talk about it:
- What is one way your spouse has loved you well this week? Thank them for that now.
- Talk about how you each prefer to receive love (you might refer to Gary Chapman's *Five Love Languages* for more understanding: for example, giving gifts, acts of service, physical touch, quality time, or words of affirmation).

Do it:
On your own, find one or two ways you can love your spouse in his or her love language this week.

PRAY FOR AND WITH EACH OTHER

WEEK 3

||||||||||

JOY

But the fruit of the Spirit is love, *joy,* peace, patience,
kindness, goodness, faithfulness, gentleness, self-control;
against such things there is no law.
GALATIANS 5:22–23 ESV

BEFORE YOU BEGIN
Take time to prepare your mind, your heart, and your space.
Be open to change; listen well and anticipate a positive experience.

START THE CONVERSATION
- What encouraged you this past week?
- What discouraged you this past week?
- What one thing can I do to help you in the week ahead?
- What are your prayer needs for the week ahead?

5-MINUTE READ-ALOUD
Ryan:

Take a moment and answer the following question for me: What brings
you joy? Seriously…stop for just a moment and do this.

Hopefully, your spouse made it on your list (after all, this is a marriage
book). But if you have kids, you may have also written their names
down. You may have listed some of your favorite hobbies, like camping,
basketball, or playing piano.

In a culture of constant connectivity, entertainment at the click of a button, and the ability to have almost everything delivered to your door, it's easy to confuse joy with happiness. I would suggest that happiness is something you *feel* or *experience* when you think of something, do something, or receive something. Happiness can be fleeting. Here today and gone tomorrow.

Joy, on the other hand, does not reflect a *feeling*. Joy is rooted in something permanent. I believe that true joy is rooted in the gospel of Jesus Christ.

In the birth account of Jesus from the Gospel of Luke, we find the beginning of true joy! We read in chapter 2 verse 10 that "the angel said to them, 'Fear not, for behold, I bring you good news of great joy that will be for all the people.'"

The good news that the angel is talking about is Jesus. His birth, life, death, and resurrection; it's the gospel. Notice how it is available to everyone. So, it's not exclusive to a feeling, a certain demographic, or a particular kind of person.

Therefore, when we talk about joy in the context of marriage, we are not talking about happiness. We are talking about something that is gospel-centric and gospel-saturated.

After the apostle Paul planted a church in the city of Thessalonica, he wrote a letter back to them offering a word of assurance and comfort. In 1 Thessalonians 1:6–7 he wrote, *"And you became imitators of us and of the Lord, for you received the word in much affliction, with the joy of the Holy Spirit, so that you became an example to all the believers in Macedonia and in Achaia."*

Did you catch that? In much affliction, or in other words, in great hardship or trials, they received the gospel, and their lives were transformed. How? Through the power of the Holy Spirit. The Holy Spirit produces joy in your life regardless of your station or circumstance. This letter was written to a church, but I believe that the application is for marriages as well. If you will yield to the Spirit working in your life, then you *will* have more joy.

Notice what happened when the Thessalonians received the word "with the joy of the Holy Spirit." The verse says that the Thessalonian example sounded forth to others in Macedonia and Achaia. The same thing is true for your marriage. When you walk in step with the Spirit, the joy in your marriage will ring out to your neighbors, coworkers, kids, parents, and friends.

Husbands and wives know this:

Happiness is temporary and is typically followed by emptiness. However, joy is eternal and is always accompanied by fulfillment.

Let me ask you: is your marriage fulfilling?

DIG DEEPER

Think about it:

- When you think about your marriage, is your foundation grounded in Jesus? If not, today may be the day you realize your marriage started out on the wrong foot. Today is the day you can start over by grounding your marriage in Jesus. Then, and only then, can joy become a fruit of your marriage.
- If your marriage *is* grounded in Jesus, then you should be experiencing the joy that comes from the Holy Spirit *within your relationship*. Can anyone else see it? Ask yourselves, is your relationship a reflection of Jesus? If so, then joy will be put on display in your marriage. Are you hiding this fruit? If so, what are you afraid of?
- Take some time to answer this question again. What brings you joy?

PRAY FOR AND WITH EACH OTHER

WEEK 4

||||||||||

KINDNESS

But the fruit of the Spirit is love, joy, peace, patience,
kindness, goodness, faithfulness, gentleness, self-control;
against such things there is no law.
GALATIANS 5:22–23 ESV

BEFORE YOU BEGIN
Take time to prepare your mind, your heart, and your space.
Be open to change; listen well and anticipate a positive experience.

START THE CONVERSATION
- What encouraged you this past week?
- What discouraged you this past week?
- What one thing can I do to help you in the week ahead?
- What are your prayer needs for the week ahead?

5-MINUTE READ-ALOUD
Jenny:
Kindness is, many times, something we reserve for the stranger asking
for directions, or our employees who show up late to a meeting, or even
our friends and acquaintances who ask insane things of us at the last
minute. It may be rare for us to exhibit kindness to our own family or to
those with whom we spend a lot of time. I have found that the closer I am
to Christ, and the more I am in his Word, the more kindness I can muster
up for strangers, but sometimes it can be difficult to show kindness to my

family—most importantly my spouse. Kindness can occasionally require a sacrifice, but most often it is as simple as offering an encouraging word, or small gesture or task, with a soft tone and a smile.

Am I showing the same kindness to my husband that I am to my best friend or neighbor? Am I seeking to understand him before I default to judgment? Do I make a conscious effort (kindness doesn't always come naturally to me) to say and do things for my spouse that are pleasing to God?

If someone drops their keys near me in a parking lot, more than likely I will pick them up for them, even if I have to stop what I am doing and go out of my way to do so. If my spouse forgets where we keep the spare grocery bags, am I willing to show him the same kindness and simply tell him, or do I go directly into attack mode, complaining that he never knows where anything is? (I may have said or thought this a time or two.)

In 2 Peter 1:5–7, Peter told us:

Make every effort to add to your faith goodness; and to goodness, knowledge; and to knowledge, self-control; and to self-control, perseverance; and to perseverance, godliness; and to godliness, mutual affection; and to mutual affection, love.

What does this have to do with kindness toward our spouses? Having self-control in how we choose to respond to our spouses is a kindness. Remembering our mutual affection, or fondness, for each other gives us more understanding when our spouses act a certain way, allowing us to show kindness through a friendly or considerate response. There is another benefit, though. By having these qualities, Peter told us in verse 8, "For if you possess these qualities in increasing measure, they will keep you from being ineffective and unproductive in your knowledge of our Lord Jesus Christ." When we know Christ more, we can better emulate him. The more we emulate him, the closer we become to our spouses.

People don't always earn, or deserve, our kindness, but if we are to imitate Christ, our spouses should be at the top of that receiving list. Again, our kindness to our spouses is not contingent on their kindness toward us. This can be hard. Sometimes we don't see or appreciate all the ways our spouses are being kind to us.

What can kindness look like in marriage? Going out of your way to show generosity and consideration to the other. Thinking about your spouse first, and being willing to sacrifice your wants and/or needs for them. Helping your spouse with things that might or might not have anything to do with you. This could be as easy as helping put away the groceries or as big as doing the actual grocery shopping. Kindness should exemplify qualities such as friendliness, consideration, and generosity. Do you approach your spouse warmly? Do you greet them with a smile? Are you considerate to your spouse when making decisions? Are you generous with kind words? Are you ready and willing to give time and effort to them on a daily basis, with a kind spirit?

Our kindness to our spouses is not contingent on their kindness toward us.

You may find it difficult to be kind to your spouse. If so, how is your relationship with the Lord? Are you reading God's Word on a consistent basis? Are you being reminded of his love for you so you can supplement your faith with all of the qualities listed in 2 Peter 1, from goodness to love? Verse 10 tells us, "if you practice these qualities, you will never fall." Kindness takes practice. If we are to imitate Christ, we need to be closely connected to him so that our marriages can better represent to the world his kindness to us.

DIG DEEPER

Think about it:
- Each of you, think of an example of God showing kindness to you this past week. During prayer time, express your gratitude to him.
- Have you noticed your spouse showing kindness to you this week? Encourage them by sharing what you noticed.
- What is one way you consider your spouse's needs or desires above your own or other family members' needs? If you can't answer this question, ask your spouse for forgiveness and make a conscious effort to reprioritize their needs.

PRAY FOR AND WITH EACH OTHER

WEEK 5

IIIIIIIII

PEACE

But the fruit of the Spirit is love, joy, ***peace,*** patience,
kindness, goodness, faithfulness, gentleness, self-control;
against such things there is no law.
Galatians 5:22–23 ESV

BEFORE YOU BEGIN
Take time to prepare your mind, your heart, and your space.
Be open to change; listen well and anticipate a positive experience.

START THE CONVERSATION
- What encouraged you this past week?
- What discouraged you this past week?
- What one thing can I do to help you in the week ahead?
- What are your prayer needs for the week ahead?

5-MINUTE READ-ALOUD
Ryan:

In Part One of *The Marriage Experience*, we looked at discipline as one
of the foundational elements of a growing, vibrant marriage. In that
devotional, I pointed you to Hebrews 12. In verse 11, we read this:

For the moment all discipline seems painful rather than pleasant,
but later it yields the peaceful fruit of righteousness to those who
have been trained by it.

Can you see the connection between discipline and peace? In this verse, we notice that peace comes from discipline. Many times, couples within the context of marriage view peace as the absence of conflict in the relationship. However, I would argue that a biblical view of peace (might I remind you that peace is a fruit of the Spirit?) includes an *attention* to conflict within your marriage. In fact, I would suggest this: *fight* for *peace* in your marriage.

Early on in our relationship, I would avoid conflict with Jenny. If she was to upset me, I would tend to bottle up my emotions, retreat for a bit, and push down anything I would want to say to her. And while you need to be careful as to how (and when) you address conflict, it is important, and scriptural, that you nurture the discipline to communicate intentionally in the midst of disagreement. In other words, do not avoid conflict—but never engage each other in a manner that is emotionally, spiritually, or physically damaging. Do your best to practice *all* the fruits, or disciplines, of the Holy Spirit as you work through your differences. This discipline produces *peace*.

You need to fight for peace in your marriage.

Continuing in Hebrews 12, when we get to verse 14 we read this: "Strive for peace with everyone, and for the holiness without which no one will see the Lord."

The verse clearly articulates that peace is not a passive byproduct when conflict is avoided. Rather, peace is something that you must *strive* after. You must work for peace. You should fight for peace.

So with this understanding, are you fighting for peace in your marriage?

DIG DEEPER

Talk about it:
- Calmly and humbly, think back to the last time you had a conflict in your marriage. Would you both agree the issue was resolved? Are there lingering feelings to address? How could you have "fought for peace" in a more disciplined and loving manner?
- Has your view of peace changed? Going forward, what would it look like to fight for peace in your marriage to achieve oneness?

PRAY FOR AND WITH EACH OTHER

WEEK 6

||||||||||

PATIENCE

But the fruit of the Spirit is love, joy, peace, *patience,*
kindness, goodness, faithfulness, gentleness, self-control;
against such things there is no law.
GALATIANS 5:22–23 ESV

BEFORE YOU BEGIN
Take time to prepare your mind, your heart, and your space.
Be open to change; listen well and anticipate a positive experience.

START THE CONVERSATION
- What encouraged you this past week?
- What discouraged you this past week?
- What one thing can I do to help you in the week ahead?
- What are your prayer needs for the week ahead?

5-MINUTE READ-ALOUD
Jenny:

Patience, oh patience. Wherefore art thou, patience? I call on patience like
I call the kids to dinner. In fact, every morning in my quiet time, I make
a point to ask God specifically for patience. I know I'm going to need it,
and I know that it is a fruit of the spirit, which means I need the power
of the Holy Spirit to get it! Why? Well for one, we have a rambunctious,
"spirited" little boy, and a lively daughter with a fifty-thousand-word daily
quota. Enough said. But even if you don't have children, think of all the

people who need your patience: the mailman (or Amazon carrier) that mishandles your package, your demanding boss, distracted coworkers or employees, the driver in front of you at the stop light that just. Won't. Turn! The fast-food cashier struggling with your order, your fretful mother—and your spouse. Yes, especially your spouse. And even though our love is limitless, our patience is not.

Patience is a thoughtful, controlled reaction to something said or done that isn't pleasing. Many days, my patience runs out before my husband even gets home from work. I have spent it all on errands, lunches, toys in the hall, and other shenanigans throughout the day. But my spouse needs my patience just as much as everyone else, if not more, because somehow he hasn't learned over all the years how to read every facial expression, gesture, and thought pattern I have! The longer we've been married, the more I have learned that we still need a lot of help strengthening our marriage, and patience is an essential part of that.

In Proverbs, Solomon (the wisest man ever—besides Jesus, of course) speaks a lot about patience. He said, "Through patience a ruler can be persuaded" (25:15) and "better a patient person than a warrior" (16:32). He spoke of how powerful patience can be. Without it, he said, we "display folly" (14:29) and "stir up conflict" (15:18).

Being patient takes forethought and intention. It takes the place of harsh words and rash reactions. It takes a moment to think about how you are going to respond to something said or done. How do you respond to your spouse at the end of the day, when your patience is lacking? Do you create conflict, or calm a quarrel? Do you show understanding or throw a tantrum? Breathe in, breathe out, count to five, ten, or a hundred, and ask God for patience so you can respond to your spouse in a respectful, loving, and appropriate way.

Being patient takes forethought and intention.

DIG DEEPER

Talk about it:

- What is one thing that drains your patience in a typical day? Ask each other how you can help in this area. Let's not forget, prayer is a powerful tool that many times is underutilized in our marriages. Asking for prayer from your spouse is one of the best ways to combat a lack of patience in any particular area.
- Talk about your patience levels during the week. When you see each other after a long day at work, where are those levels? Are some days going to be worse than others? Sharing this information with your spouse helps each of you be more proactive about not stressing each other out on those days—and helps you anticipate their needs.
- What is the one area in which you can see that you try your spouse's patience most often? Talk about something that you can do to help each other in this area.

PRAY FOR AND WITH EACH OTHER

WEEK 7

||||||||||

FAITHFULNESS

But the fruit of the Spirit is love, joy, peace, patience,
kindness, goodness, *faithfulness,* gentleness, self-control;
against such things there is no law.
GALATIANS 5:22–23 ESV

BEFORE YOU BEGIN
Take time to prepare your mind, your heart, and your space.
Be open to change; listen well and anticipate a positive experience.

START THE CONVERSATION
- What encouraged you this past week?
- What discouraged you this past week?
- What one thing can I do to help you in the week ahead?
- What are your prayer needs for the week ahead?

5-MINUTE READ-ALOUD
Ryan:

Have you ever sincerely thought about faithfulness? Pause and take a
moment to do that.

As you spent some time doing that, you may have thought through a
few questions:

- What is the difference between faith and faithfulness?
- How is faithfulness a fruit of the Spirit?

- How does this apply to marriage?

Let's tackle some of these questions to bring some clarity regarding faithfulness.

What is the difference between faith and faithfulness? Faith is to believe in or put your trust in something or someone. In the context of Christianity, faith is to believe in God. Faith is to believe in Jesus Christ. Faith is to place your trust in Jesus as Lord and Savior of your life.

Faithfulness, on the other hand, is the fruit that comes from faith. To be faithful is to be committed to believe and trust in God. Faithfulness is to behave in a way that affirms your faith.

Next, how is faithfulness a fruit of the Spirit?

In the context of Galatians 5:22–23, we know that faithfulness is a personal fruit in one's life that reveals the Spirit of God living within them. It is extremely important to understand that you cannot grow in faithfulness on your own. A believer's faithfulness grows because of the Holy Spirit.

This should give you great hope and it should be a source of gratitude in your life! Because he is faithful, we too can be faithful!

Finally, how does faithfulness apply to marriage?

First, and this may be a hard truth for you, you cannot be truly faithful in your marriage unless you are first faithful to God. And when I say, "be truly faithful in your marriage," I do not restrict that to mean that you will not commit adultery. Faithfulness in your marriage and being faithful to your spouse goes much deeper than the basic understanding that you will not break your marriage covenant by committing adultery. Faithfulness is a commitment to love them the way that Jesus loves you. Because of your faith in Jesus, you commit to love your spouse sacrificially and extravagantly. And based on what the Bible teaches, you are to be faithful to your spouse emotionally and sexually.

You cannot be truly faithful in your marriage unless you are first faithful to God.

With this understanding, that your faithfulness to your spouse must be grounded in your faith, how might that change the way you treat your spouse?

DIG DEEPER

Think about it:
- Thinking about the Galatians 5:22–23 standard for faithfulness, are you emotionally faithful to your spouse? Are you sexually faithful? If not, today is the day for a new beginning.
- Are there any areas where you feel as if your spouse is being emotionally or sexually unfaithful to you? Have a safe, loving, honest conversation about it.

Do it:
This week, find one way you could sacrificially and extravagantly affirm your faithfulness to your spouse, and do it.

PRAY FOR AND WITH EACH OTHER

WEEK 8

||||||||||

GOODNESS

But the fruit of the Spirit is love, joy, peace, patience,
kindness, **goodness,** faithfulness, gentleness, self-control;
against such things there is no law.
GALATIANS 5:22–23 ESV

BEFORE YOU BEGIN
Take time to prepare your mind, your heart, and your space.
Be open to change; listen well and anticipate a positive experience.

START THE CONVERSATION
- What encouraged you this past week?
- What discouraged you this past week?
- What one thing can I do to help you in the week ahead?
- What are your prayer needs for the week ahead?

5-MINUTE READ-ALOUD
Jenny:

If there were ever an overused word in the English language, it would probably be *good.* Our food is "good." Our day was "good." We feel "good." We had a "good" time. Those are "good" people. That is a "good" restaurant. *Everything* can be good. Good. Good. Good. On the surface, the term *good* seems pretty mundane, so why is "goodness" a fruit of the Holy Spirit? That seems like a trait we can figure out on our own. I think there are plenty of good people in this world, and Christians certainly cannot claim to own goodness, right? So I ask again, why is "goodness" a fruit of the Holy Spirit? Is this "goodness" something different? And how can I present myself as "good" when it comes to my spouse?

For this, I had to get technical. I had to do some research, mostly because I had no clue what the answers were. I considered goodness to have similar, if not redundant, qualities to kindness (friendly, generous, considerate). I found out that goodness has its own distinct qualities that we should give special attention to. Let's look at the very beginning of God's Word, in Genesis 1. The first time the word "good" is used in the Bible is right at the beginning of creation:

"God saw that the light was good, and he separated the light from the darkness." Genesis 1:4

God spoke light into existence so his perfect creation could be revealed to the senses, and he saw that it was good. "Good" in this context meant being without blemish, without disorder, without threatening attributes. No evil. Only good. So, while this word seems simple, it actually holds a lot more value than we give it.

Now, when I think of the virtue of goodness, I think of being without blemish, disorder, or darkness. I can't help but ask myself, "Am I these things? Am I good to my husband?" The short answer? No—not always. Hence the need for the Holy Spirit. I need the power of the Holy Spirit so that I can act in accordance with goodness every. Single. Day.

Without blemish? Nope. Not me. But with the power of the Holy Spirit, which I received when I put my entire faith and trust in the Lord, I *can* be without blemish. Let's not rush past that. When you put your entire faith and trust in the Lord, you receive the Holy Spirit, and you have the power of God in you. Trust it. Use it.

But, like all of the other fruits of the Spirit, I have to desire it, ask for it, and intentionally display this behavior when I am confronted with the choice to choose goodness or choose darkness. When I am confronted with the option to respond to my husband in a good way or a hurtful way. When I am faced with disappointment, I can choose to respond with goodness. Let's not forget that just because the power of the Holy Spirit is in us doesn't mean the fruit of goodness will automatically present itself in our behaviors. If that were the case, our marriages would have far less challenges, because the fruit of the Spirit would be displayed constantly. If we live by the Spirit of God, we must "keep in step with the spirit" as Galatians 5:25 states. This requires conscious intent and desire.

Keeping in step with the Spirit requires conscious intent and desire. It doesn't "just happen."

The light was good—it allowed a perfect creation to be seen. If a light were shown on our marriages, would it show a perfect creation? Make an effort the next time you pray to ask for a good spirit toward your spouse, and trust that he will empower and enable you to have just that. The next time you are asked about your day, don't just say it was "good." Chances are, it probably wasn't Galatians 5:22 good!

DIG DEEPER

Think about it:
- Where is there darkness creeping in your marriage? Take your time answering this. Perhaps something in your marriage is out of order, out of alignment, or off track. Is the Holy Spirit pricking you about anything?
- If a light were shown on how you treat your spouse, what would it reveal?

Talk about it:
Talk about something this week that showed a lack of goodness in your marriage or how you treated each other. Talk about how to prevent or overcome that in the future.

PRAY FOR AND WITH EACH OTHER

WEEK 9

||||||||||

SELF-CONTROL

But the fruit of the Spirit is love, joy, peace, patience,
kindness, goodness, faithfulness, gentleness, *self-control;*
against such things there is no law.
Galatians 5:22–23 ESV

BEFORE YOU BEGIN
Take time to prepare your mind, your heart, and your space.
Be open to change; listen well and anticipate a positive experience.

START THE CONVERSATION
- What encouraged you this past week?
- What discouraged you this past week?
- What one thing can I do to help you in the week ahead?
- What are your prayer needs for the week ahead?

5-MINUTE READ-ALOUD
Ryan:

Self-control is the final fruit of the Spirit listed in Galatians 5:22–23.
I think most understand the importance of self-control, yet if we are
honest, we recognize many of us can talk the talk but find it hard to walk
the walk in this area.

The Bible is filled with verses that exhort its readers to practice
self-control. With this in mind, we can infer a couple things about
self-control as it relates to our marriages:

- **There is something inside *all* of us that needs to be restrained, disciplined, or bridled.**

You must come to grips with this for yourself, and for your spouse. We are all sinners (Romans 3:23). All of us are in need of the grace of God. Your spouse has temptations that they struggle with, and you are not perfect, either. Take the time right now to identify those areas where you struggle, and share those areas with your spouse.

- **There is a way to grow in self-control.**

Despite the word "self" in self-control, it actually begins apart from yourself. Ultimately, self-control comes with a complete dependence upon God. It's only after you come to the end of yourself that you can find Jesus. And Jesus is the only answer to truly bridle the sinful desires that can run rampant in our lives.

Ultimately, self-control comes with a complete dependence upon God.

DIG DEEPER

Think about it:
- How can you come alongside your spouse to aid them in self-control?
- What area(s) in your life need the most attention concerning self-control?

PRAY FOR AND WITH EACH OTHER

WEEK 10

||||||||||

GENTLENESS

But the fruit of the Spirit is love, joy, peace, patience,
kindness, goodness, faithfulness, ***gentleness,*** self-control;
against such things there is no law.
GALATIANS 5:22–23 ESV

BEFORE YOU BEGIN
Take time to prepare your mind, your heart, and your space.
Be open to change; listen well and anticipate a positive experience.

START THE CONVERSATION
- What encouraged you this past week?
- What discouraged you this past week?
- What one thing can I do to help you in the week ahead?
- What are your prayer needs for the week ahead?

5-MINUTE READ-ALOUD
Jenny:

As I write this, a newborn was recently born into this family. This sweet
baby girl was in the NICU the first two weeks of her life, and Ryan and I
had the rare and beautiful privilege of visiting her. The moment I stepped
into the ward, I tried to do everything with at least ten times more finesse
than usual. The way I spoke, the way I retrieved my ID from my wallet,
the way that I walked. And all that increased even more when I tiptoed
into her room. We spoke in hushed tones, and we handled her with such

care so as not to disturb her or any of the mass of wires monitoring her. In a word, we were gentle.

In Proverbs, Solomon told us that a soft (gentle) answer turns away anger (15:1) and allows us to be heard. In Philippians, Paul said that we are to let our reasonableness (gentleness) be evident and known to all (4:5).

At home, gentleness doesn't mean tiptoeing or whispering (unless we have a newborn, of course). So, how do we present the gentleness that is spoken of in Scripture? How do we respond when our spouse asks (for the third time) where something is? Is our tone gentle when we are running out the door to an activity or event and our spouse asks us to do something for them before we go?

Let's think for a moment about all of the fruits of the Holy Spirit. Are you noticing that these fruits work much better together? If we battle with one particular discipline, there may be a companion fruit (or two) that also challenges us. Self-control and faithfulness. Kindness and goodness. If we struggle with patience, we probably also struggle with gentleness. Likewise, the more we work on our patience, the gentler we are, and vice versa. If my first reaction to a circumstance is exasperation instead of patience, my response is much more likely to be short and ill-tempered than gentle.

Remember to think of the fruits of the Holy Spirit as disciplines. We think of fruit as a crop we can harvest once it ripens on the vine—but the fruit of the Holy Spirit doesn't ripen on its own. These are disciplines. These are choices. It's worth repeating that choosing to exhibit these fruits is difficult. *Gentleness* is difficult. Last week, Ryan described self-control as an outpouring of our dependence on God. It's the same with all of the fruits of the Spirit, including gentleness. On our own, we cannot muster up the strength we need to be gentle with our spouses all the time. As Romans 8:26 states, "the Spirit helps us in our weakness," even interceding for us when we pray.

The next time you feel a harsh answer welling up within you, take a pause. Ask the Lord to give you a gentle word so that you can respond in a way that will turn away anger, but still allow you to be heard.

DIG DEEPER

Think about it:

- When is it most difficult for you to treat your spouse with gentleness? Why do you think that is?
- When is it easiest to be gentle with each other? Why do you think that is?

Talk about it:

Consider all the fruits, or disciplines, from the past ten weeks. Take turns sharing which is the greatest challenge within your marriage right now. Pray about it together. Then, this week, be intentional about practicing that particular discipline.

PRAY FOR AND WITH EACH OTHER

WEEK 11

||||||||||

SANCTIFICATION

BEFORE YOU BEGIN

Take time to prepare your mind, your heart, and your space.
Be open to change; listen well and anticipate a positive experience.

START THE CONVERSATION

- What encouraged you this past week?
- What discouraged you this past week?
- What one thing can I do to help you in the week ahead?
- What are your prayer needs for the week ahead?

5-MINUTE READ-ALOUD

Ryan:

We've spent ten weeks talking about how the work of the Holy Spirit, the fruit, applies to our lives and our marriage relationships. We reminded you that it takes dependence on God for these fruits to develop—and lots of time. This ripening of our spiritual fruit is called *sanctification*. After entering into a relationship with Jesus, sanctification is the lifelong process through which the Holy Spirit changes you to look more like Jesus. During this process you bear fruit from the indwelling of the Holy Spirit in your life (Galatians 5:22–23). But in addition to this, husbands play an important role in the sanctification of their wives. Read Ephesians 5:25–26:

Husbands, love your wives, as Christ loved the church and gave himself up for her, that he might sanctify her, having cleansed her by the washing of water with the word.

In the context of this passage, we see again that marriage is to be a picture of the relationship between Jesus and the church (his bride). And under the umbrella of loving our wives, we husbands are also told to sanctify our wives. This sounds like a tremendous responsibility, and it is.

So, husbands, are you doing this? Do you understand what it means to sanctify your wife? Wives, do you allow your husband to aid in this process? Husbands, are you conducting your life in such a way that you also are being sanctified?

Ephesians 5:25–26 states that husbands are to bring about sanctification in their wives through their love and sacrifice. It's a scary thing to know that you are partly responsible for your wife's spiritual maturity, but God has great purpose in this. You see, when we care about the spiritual growth of someone else, God will use that to bring about spiritual growth in our own lives.

Husbands, how do you do this? While I don't have an exhaustive list, let me give you a few suggestions.

First: set the example. Regularly seek after Jesus, and your wife will notice.

Second: set a regular time to talk about what Jesus is doing in your lives, just the two of you. This book was created for this very purpose, so I think you are headed in the right direction.

Last: set spiritual goals as a couple. Lean in to God, and seek his voice. A spiritual goal might include looking for a small group or class to join at church, attending a retreat, going through a book or Bible study together, joining a ministry, or going on a short-term mission trip together, for example. The result of a joint goal for Jenny and me was to write a book, and from that point until the publishing of this book, God has been sanctifying us both!

**Set spiritual goals as a couple.
Lean in to God, and seek his voice.**

DIG DEEPER

Think about it:

- Think about your habitual spiritual activity in your home. This is where sanctification begins! What does your devotional time, or your quiet time, look like? Are you regularly reading God's Word? Do you pray often? If not, plan a regular time, beginning tomorrow, to refresh these disciplines in your home.
- Wives, how open are you to your husband's spiritual leadership? Hopefully you now have a better understanding of his responsibility for you in this area. How can you affirm and encourage his efforts?

Do it:

Set at least one spiritual goal as a couple. Choose a goal for the two of you together, and only the two of you.

PRAY FOR AND WITH EACH OTHER

WEEK 12

||||||||||

SERVICE

BEFORE YOU BEGIN
Take time to prepare your mind, your heart, and your space.
Be open to change; listen well and anticipate a positive experience.

START THE CONVERSATION
- What encouraged you this past week?
- What discouraged you this past week?
- What one thing can I do to help you in the week ahead?
- What are your prayer needs for the week ahead?

5-MINUTE READ-ALOUD
Jenny:

You've experienced nine different disciplines that can be game-changers for your marriage (one of them twice!). The natural result of enjoying this fruit in your life is that you become sanctified together as a couple. You are drawing closer and closer to the relationship you desire. The next natural step is an outward expression of that growth: service.

As believers in Christ, we have two great commandments: love God, and love others (Matthew 22:37–39 paraphrased). And with that love, serve them with the gifts that we've been given by God. In marriages, it's so easy to forget sometimes that our spouse is a part of those "others." In fact, our spouse is the *primary* "other" that should receive our love and, therefore, our service.

Service looks different to different people simply because we have all been given a variety of gifts. What are your unique gifts, and how can you use them to serve your spouse in the best way?

For example, I am not a great cook. I'm an OK cook, and I don't mind saying that creating gorgeous, delicious meals is not a gift of mine. However, I have been given a gift of resourcefulness, so one way I serve Ryan is by taking initiative in repairing things in our home (or calling a professional when I know I can't. Trust me, that's service!).

Ryan has a gift of financial knowledge and discernment. One way he serves me is handling the bills, budget, and security of our finances, which serves me greatly! I always say he is the reason we have money in the bank!

These are *natural* gifts; some would call them talents that we have been given by God through our parents and upbringing. More importantly, we also have gifts given to us by God through the Holy Spirit. These are called our *spiritual* gifts, and are wholly separate from our natural talents and the fruit of the Spirit we've just spent so many weeks learning about. If you don't already know your spiritual gifts, start learning about them through the Bible, particularly 1 Corinthians 12 and Romans 12. Using all of our gifts to serve our spouses is equally as important as using them to serve the church.

My top spiritual gifts are giving and encouragement. Since Ryan's career is serving the church, I serve Ryan best with my spiritual gifts by giving my time and talents freely and cheerfully to the work and mission of the church. This also helps me be patient when his calling and responsibilities pull him away from his family, but sometimes encouragement means I gently help him keep balance in his life, which can be a struggle for him. (Let's be honest—I'm not always gentle!) I also serve him by encouraging him in his leadership calling within the church. Daily, I pray for his effectiveness and am excited to watch God work in and through him.

Ryan's spiritual gifts are shepherding and leadership, which probably makes sense after that last paragraph. He serves me well by leading me to accomplish my spiritual goals and caring for me spiritually. He encourages and initiates time in our home to devote to prayer and worship on a consistent basis, shepherding and leading our family.

I know it can be difficult, especially after a long day of serving others, to serve each other with our remaining few hours of the day. However, serving our spouses is a crucial way we can show our love and affection, and is easier when we use our God-given gifts.

I also realize that some of us become paralyzed with the thought that we are not talented enough to serve *well*. "Why serve at all?" we ask ourselves. We watch others serve with such excellence, we become defeated and hesitant even to try. We think we aren't capable—we sell ourselves short. This is an outright lie that the enemy would *love* to put in our heads. He wants to keep us from serving our spouses and having exceptional marriages. Think of service as a muscle: the more you work it, the more capable it gets. Practice serving your spouse in small, intentional ways, and watch that muscle grow!

> **Serving our spouses is a crucial way we can show our love and affection, and is easier when we use our God-given gifts.**

DIG DEEPER

Talk about it:
- What are your natural and spiritual gifts? If you do not know, ask your spouse—they may see them in you.
- How are you using your gifts to serve your spouse? If you struggle to find an answer, be intentional this week about employing your gifts to strengthen and lift up your spouse. Pay attention to the difference it makes.
- Take a moment to communicate to your spouse that you are grateful for their service to you. Thank each other for one specific way they have served you recently.

PRAY FOR AND WITH EACH OTHER

WEEK 13

||||||||||||

CELEBRATION

BEFORE YOU BEGIN

Take time to prepare your mind, your heart, and your space.
Be open to change; listen well and anticipate a positive experience.

START THE CONVERSATION

- What encouraged you this past week?
- What discouraged you this past week?
- What one thing can I do to help you in the week ahead?
- What are your prayer needs for the week ahead?

5-MINUTE READ-ALOUD

You did it! By the end of this week, you will have completed Parts One and Two of *The Marriage Experience*. You will have spent at least twenty-six weeks—that's half of a *year*—investing time in your marriage, working together, and having meaningful, deep conversations to build the relationship you both desire! You are starting to build muscle memory, strong, life-giving habits, and you are growing closer to each other and closer to God. That's amazing! Now that you are finished with the second part of *The Marriage Experience*, it's time again to celebrate! We have outlined a few options below to give you a kick-start.

DIG DEEPER

Reflect on it: We covered some difficult ground together. You may have unearthed some uncomfortable truths. You may have realized new and wonderful things about each other. Sum up your thoughts about the experience in a few words or phrases, and write it down where you can see it. Encourage each other in what you just accomplished together by sharing your thoughts.

Share it: Share what you've learned with another couple, your small group, or even a quick social media post. Remember the strength found in accountability! Encourage other couples to start this same journey.

Do it: Plan something special together to celebrate in the week ahead. It's time for a date! It's time to make a memory!

Show it: Show the world, or at least your community, that you are on fire for God and each other. Continue to put Jesus on display through your marriage, flaws and all. Remember, no marriage is perfect. Seeing your honesty and commitment to build a deeper, Spirit-centered relationship will spark an interest in someone else that could lead to gospel conversations.

Write it: Write each other a letter sharing your gratitude for their interest in your marriage. That would be a great place for encouragement and continued affection.

Dream it: Take a moment and dream together. Look how far you have come, and talk about where you want your marriage to go next.

Give it: Give your loved one a little token of your affection. It does not have to be a big gesture or cost a lot of money. Let it be a reminder of this shared experience.

Continue it: Read the intro to the next unit and hit the gas!

PRAY FOR AND WITH EACH OTHER

PART THREE//FRIENDSHIP

||||||||||

DID YOU KNOW THERE is a strong connection between the best aspects of friendship and the marriage relationship? Doesn't that sound fun? In Part Three//Friendship, each week we will look at a different aspect of friendship—okay, one week we will depart a bit when we talk about romance…and sex! You know you want to talk about it (or need to). You will be surprised and delighted to learn how much you already know about friendship, what the Bible says about friends, and how to bring out those qualities to strengthen your marriage. After all, your spouse can and should be your friend too! There will be some deep dives along the way, important conversations to prepare you for your future (which, by the way, is the subject of the fourth and final part of *The Marriage Experience*). You're doing great! Your commitment to each other is breath-taking!

Part One should have widened your understanding of what your marriage is really all about (hint: it's *not* about you). Part Two hopefully connected you more fully to the greatest power you have working for you. Along with lots of encouraging conversation starters, Part Three may also reveal some spots in your relationship that need a little tune-up. With just a little work, your marriage ride will be so much smoother. As before, we designed this series in a twelve-week unit, closing with suggestions for an enjoyable celebration activity. Make each week's time a priority; deflect interruptions. If you are unable to complete a week, do not skip it. Pick up where you left off as soon as you are able.

Let's start the conversation—Part Three!

Ryan and Jenny

WEEK 1

|||||||||

GRATITUDE

BEFORE YOU BEGIN
Take time to prepare your mind, your heart, and your space.
Be open to change; listen well and anticipate a positive experience.

START THE CONVERSATION
- What encouraged you this past week?
- What discouraged you this past week?
- What one thing can I do to help you in the week ahead?
- What are your prayer needs for the week ahead?

5-MINUTE READ-ALOUD
Jenny:

Normally I don't start these guides with a definition because, frankly, I can assume that, if you are reading this book, you don't need clarification about the meaning of basic vocabulary. But, as we have seen with the previous two parts of *The Marriage Experience*, sometimes a word can have different applications, different meanings. As simple as it seems, now is the time we all need to be on the same page with that word: gratitude. Gratitude is not just being thankful. It is also "readiness to *show* appreciation for and to *return* kindness," according to the New Oxford American Dictionary. Did you get that last part?

Gratitude is readiness to show appreciation and to return kindness.

I have a friend I meet regularly for coffee. I remember the first time, she was adamant that she pay for my drink. It was so thoughtful, I made certain to get hers the next time—not out of obligation, but as a response to her kindness. We've now been buying each other's drinks for about two years. You see, gratitude isn't just a two-way street where someone does or says something kind, the other person says "thank you," and it's over. It's more like a roundabout in an intersection (I know, I hate those too, but it's the best analogy I have): someone does or says something kind, the other person does or says something to show appreciation and kindness in return, and then that person returns with more gratitude. For gratitude to be sincere, by definition, it should never end. If Ryan does something nice for me and I just say "thank you" without a kindness in return, the "traffic" stops until someone does something kind again further down the road (pun intended).

There is power in a simple thank-you when it comes to our marriages. Saying those words acknowledges that something kind was done and appreciated. Saying thank you also promotes positivity in your marriage. Think of how hearing those words makes you feel. Feeling appreciated leads to more acts of kindness. More acts of kindness result in more gratitude. There's that roundabout again! Without the "roundabout of gratitude" in our marriages, we run the risk of having negative acts and feelings override the positive. Let's face it—every marriage has negative moments creep in from time to time. But, with gratitude going around and around, those negative situations will have a much smaller impact on the relationship as a whole.

How can gratitude look in your marriage? Besides saying the words "thank you," showing appreciation might mean writing a note or sending a text, acknowledging a nice thing has been done. And while I encourage saying thank you shortly after receiving an act of kindness, sometimes gratitude can and should be expressed much later, as part of a *continual expression* of gratitude. For example, Ryan sometimes makes my coffee in the morning. He only started doing that after we had been married at least ten years, so to say I'm thankful for this kindness is an understatement. Do I say thank you every time he makes it, even though it's something he does frequently? Of course! But I also have sent him a text randomly in the week letting him know I'm thankful when he makes my coffee—as a continual expression of gratitude.

Returning kindness might mean finding something your spouse does routinely, and doing it for them—or sending them a kind word in the middle of a work day, or when they have to work late, letting them know you are thinking of them, or to encourage them. Regardless of how you show your gratitude, showing your spouse you love them and appreciate them must be a regular presence in your marriage.

DIG DEEPER

Share it:
Thank each other for one or two kindnesses you have heard or received from your spouse this week. Then, think of a kindness your spouse does frequently that perhaps you haven't acknowledged in a while.

Pray about it:
Take turns in prayer thanking God for the relationship you have with him, and with each other. Be specific when you pray, being thankful that your spouse sees your needs and responds in loving acts of kindness.

PRAY FOR AND WITH EACH OTHER

WEEK 2

||||||||||

HONESTY

BEFORE YOU BEGIN
Take time to prepare your mind, your heart, and your space.
Be open to change; listen well and anticipate a positive experience.

START THE CONVERSATION
- What encouraged you this past week?
- What discouraged you this past week?
- What one thing can I do to help you in the week ahead?
- What are your prayer needs for the week ahead?

5-MINUTE READ-ALOUD
Ryan:

As a dad, there are two things that my kids do (just like all kids) that really frustrate me: when they lie, and when they are lazy. Since I was a child, I've always had an issue with people not telling the truth (unfortunately, just like everyone else, I have struggled with this). If you are truly my friend, then you will be honest with me, even if it hurts.

In Proverbs 6:16–19 we are told "there are six things that the Lord hates, seven that are an abomination to him." Included in that passage is "a lying tongue."

In Philippians 4:8, the apostle Paul told his readers to think on things are worthy of praise; things that are true fall into that category.

In John 8:32, Jesus said, "And you will know the truth, and the truth will set you free."

The Bible is full of verses that address honesty and telling the truth. I believe that being honest with your spouse is a necessity when it comes to putting the gospel on display, and also having a vibrant marriage. You see, so many of the topics that we will cover in Part Three regarding friendship are grounded in honesty. Romance, trust, loyalty, sacrifice— these things cannot truly exist in a closed-off, deceitful marriage.

It's important to note that when we speak of honesty, we are not just relegating honesty to mean "*not* telling lies." True honesty also means opening up and being transparent with your spouse. Do you have something that you are hiding from your spouse? It could be a feeling, a habit, a relationship, something from your past, or something that just happened. What is God nudging you to be honest about right now? James 4:17 says: "So whoever knows the right thing to do and fails to do it, for him it is sin."

It's far easier to "be honest" with our spouses about their own faults and failures, and accountability is an important aspect of marriage, but today let's humbly focus on ourselves. If you know it is right to confess something to your spouse, then you need to do it. Husbands, if you are like me, then this can be a difficult thing. My pride will cloud my judgment and cause me to keep my faults and failures to myself. But if you really want your marriage to thrive, you must speak the truth—even when it means revealing your own weaknesses.

If you know it is right to confess something to your spouse, then you need to do it.

Within your marriage:

- vulnerable, transparent honesty frees you from feeling isolated.
- vulnerable, transparent honesty frees you from the pressure that comes from bottling things up.
- vulnerable, transparent honesty frees you from having to pretend to be perfect.

Again, the truth will set you free.

DIG DEEPER

Talk about it:
- In what areas in your marriage do you find it most difficult be honest?
- What is the primary reason you fail to be completely transparent with your spouse?
- Do you still feel guilty for a past act of deceit? How might you find a path to reconciliation in your marriage?

PRAY FOR AND WITH EACH OTHER

WEEK 3

|||||||||

PRIORITY

BEFORE YOU BEGIN

Take time to prepare your mind, your heart, and your space.
Be open to change; listen well and anticipate a positive experience.

START THE CONVERSATION

- What encouraged you this past week?
- What discouraged you this past week?
- What one thing can I do to help you in the week ahead?
- What are your prayer needs for the week ahead?

5-MINUTE READ-ALOUD

Jenny:

My dearest childhood friend and I were inseparable. We were completely different in so many ways but loved spending all our time together. As we grew, our friendship became less important than other interests, other people. Our time together was no longer a priority. We drifted apart, as some childhood friendships do.

What are your priorities? Here's a good test: what ends up at the top of your list on a day-to-day, week-to-week, and month-to-month basis? In other words, what do you make sure to schedule time for? Does your spouse occupy any slots on your list? If I were to ask them if they were on your priority list, would they respond with an emphatic yes? Would they shrug their shoulders and utter, "I guess"? Or would they flat-out say no? Do you feel you make the top of your spouse's non-negotiable list of priorities? Or do you feel you are drifting apart?

Here is the thing about priorities: everyone has them and it's usually quite simple to identify them for yourself. I know you are reading a guide about marriage, but bear with me for a moment. Who should be our ultimate priority? You might have guessed it: God. But, do we make time for him? Our relationship with Christ is generally reflected in our relationship with our spouse (and a slew of other people). I know that when I am in the Word daily and talking with God "without ceasing" as the apostle Paul instructed us in 1 Thessalonians 5:17 (ESV), my relationship with Ryan reflects that same consistency. In other words, when I make a daily priority of spending time with God, I find that I also make a daily priority of connecting and communicating with my husband. I consider him first. I think about what he would want, or what he needs. God wants us to put him first, with all our "soul, mind, and strength." After that, he commands us to love our neighbor:

> Jesus replied: "'Love the Lord your God with all your heart and with all your soul and with all your mind.' This is the first and greatest commandment. And the second is like it: 'Love your neighbor as yourself.' All the Law and the Prophets hang on these two commandments." Matthew 22:37–40

Think of your spouse as your closest neighbor. Not your children, not your parents, not your best friend—your spouse. Are you diligent in showing that? Are you being diligent in showing God he is your number one priority?

One crucial way I put God first is with a morning quiet time, especially before I check email or social media. It's in that time with him that he affirms my abilities as a wife and a mother and sets my mind and heart right for the day ahead. It's so easy to push that aside, but keeping consistent in my quiet time shows God his place in my life.

A few ways that Ryan and I put each other first are with overnight getaways once a quarter, weekly dates going to coffee, and weeknight connection after the kids go to bed. I know this isn't possible in every season (it certainly wasn't for us), but we have worked hard to make adjustments that put our marriage (and each other) first.

Putting God first and our spouses second means that if we have children, they come third. I know this can be really difficult—after all, you only have eighteen years with them (ok, perhaps a few more), and once they're gone they are likely gone forever (cue the tears). I get it, but your children will also need to put their spouses first someday, and one of the best ways they will learn to do that is if you model it for them. We made sure to do this when our kids were young, but it's never too late to start. Building a new priority when so many other obligations have had the top spot for a while might be a bit challenging, but don't let the difficulty deter you. Prioritizing God, then your spouse, is vital to a thriving marriage.

> **Putting God first and our spouses second means that everyone and everything else follows.**

For us, the conversation with our kids went something like this: "We love you so much. But guess what? We loved each other first, and will need to love each other still when you are on your own. That's why we need our time to talk and hang out when you go to bed. So, at bedtime, you are not to leave your room unless it's an emergency—for example, you're bleeding, barfing, or on fire! [Pause for dramatic effect.] Kids, this is really important to us." This might seem difficult, but once our oldest understood the importance of our time together, she was (mostly) obedient and respectful of it. It's not always picture-perfect, but it shows our respect for our time together—and provides an important model for our kiddos!

DIG DEEPER

Talk about it:
How are you doing with your time in prayer and studying God's Word? He should be our ultimate priority and growing closer to him will allow us to grow closer to our spouses. If you are not yet consistently spending time with God, that needs to be your first step. Like seriously, start tomorrow.

Do it:

When is the last time you and your spouse went on a date? Do you already date regularly? Good for you! When is the last time you had a night *without* the kids? If it's been too long, or if you are not consistent with either of these, plan a date night, afternoon, or weekend right now. Go ahead and put it on the calendar. We'll wait...

Great job! Here's the kicker: stick to it. Don't let other plans come before these dates. They are non-negotiables!

PRAY FOR AND WITH EACH OTHER

WEEK 4

||||||||||

AFFIRMATION

BEFORE YOU BEGIN
Take time to prepare your mind, your heart, and your space.
Be open to change; listen well and anticipate a positive experience.

START THE CONVERSATION
- What encouraged you this past week?
- What discouraged you this past week?
- What one thing can I do to help you in the week ahead?
- What are your prayer needs for the week ahead?

5-MINUTE READ-ALOUD

Ryan:

I had a friend in high school who never failed to build me up every time they saw me. They were always genuinely glad to see me and gave me a great big smile that said, "Ryan, you are the best!" Whatever I did, they were among the first to congratulate me, encourage me, or lift me up if I was struggling. In other words, they were very affirming.

Have you read Gary Chapman's book *The Five Love Languages*? If not, you should get a copy and read through it with your spouse. If you have, then you know that Chapman breaks down into five categories the ways spouses show and receive love. While I won't list them all here, one that really jumped out at me was "words of affirmation." I receive love most through words of affirmation. When Jenny tells me that I am a good husband, or when I hear one of my kids say that I am good dad, I feel loved.

Affirmation focuses in on *who* your spouse is, specifically a particular character trait you admire or want to encourage, and then may give specific details as to *how* your spouse manifested that character trait through action or word.

Affirmation is an essential component to a healthy marriage. When you affirm your spouse, both publicly and privately, you are giving support and encouragement. You are showing love. When your marriage is rooted in friendship, a natural outflow of that friendship should manifest itself through affirmation.

That friend from high school? You may have guessed it. I married her.

One of my favorite things that God says in the Bible is an affirmation. In Matthew 3:17 (also in Mark 1:11 and Luke 3:22), we read how God the Father says to Jesus the Son: "This is my beloved Son, with whom I am well pleased."

Jesus, who is God incarnate, receives affirmation from God, the Father. Jesus, who is sinless and perfect, receives affirmation from God. Jesus, who is the definition of humility, receives affirmation from God. Why? Because there is a relationship there.

If God set the example when he affirmed Jesus at the beginning of his ministry, then don't you think affirmation is crucial when it comes to your most important earthly relationship—that being your spouse?

> **If God set the example when he affirmed Jesus at the beginning of his ministry, then don't you think affirmation is crucial when it comes to your most important earthly relationship?**

So that begs the question: what does affirmation look like in your marriage?

DIG DEEPER

Talk about it:

- When is the last time you affirmed your spouse? What did you say or do?
- When was the last time your spouse said or did something affirming to you? How did receiving that affirmation make you feel?
- Take turns giving each other a word of affirmation right now. Focus in on *who* your spouse is, and then give specific details as to *how* that character trait has been manifested through action or word.

PRAY FOR AND WITH EACH OTHER

WEEK 5

||||||||||

ACCEPTANCE

BEFORE YOU BEGIN

Take time to prepare your mind, your heart, and your space.
Be open to change; listen well and anticipate a positive experience.

START THE CONVERSATION

- What encouraged you this past week?
- What discouraged you this past week?
- What one thing can I do to help you in the week ahead?
- What are your prayer needs for the week ahead?

5-MINUTE READ-ALOUD

Jenny:

Do you remember what it was like on your first day in a new school, or walking into a new church for the first time? You may have worried about what to wear, whether you would know anyone, who you'd be sitting beside. Whether you are one to hang back and stay in the shadows or jump in boldly, we all want the same thing: to be accepted. I recently reconnected with an old friend from school. The first thing we both noticed, I am sure, was that we had both changed—a lot!

Are you living with the same person you married? And no, I am not asking if you are living with someone other than your spouse. I mean, does the person you married still have the exact same qualities and personality they had when you first got married? That's kind of a trick question, isn't it? Unless you got married yesterday or last week, the answer is most likely a resounding no! We could argue whether or not those changes are a good thing, but they are definitely natural. According to Tim Keller in *The Meaning of Marriage*, we all change within the context of marriage—often many times—and that is to be expected.

Yet, wives, how many times do we look at our husbands and reflect back on the person he used to be? Husbands, how many times do you wonder where the woman you married went, or how she got to be who she is today? Despite how you feel about your spouse's changes, you must come to a place of acceptance in order to fulfill, in a loving way, your "until death do us part" commitment to each other.

When I turned thirty-eight (not that long ago) I had a moment, a reality check in the mirror, when I reminisced about the way I looked even ten years prior: less wrinkled, no gray hair (I have a few now) and a smaller pants size. But even more than that, I looked back and could see the changes in me personally—some made intentionally, others forced upon me by life situations: becoming a parent, changing jobs, moving several times, and more. The truth is, I have changed a lot since I married Ryan at the ripe old age of twenty! I'm so thankful he still loves me for who I am today, but I'm even more thankful that he seeks to better understand the "me" I am becoming.

Rather than just accepting your spouse for who he or she is today, we must accept the fact that change is inevitable. But what do we do with that knowledge? We must keep up! How? By intentionally learning about our spouses as the days and years go on. By not dwelling in the past as if your best days are behind you, but looking forward to a future together where you are both better together because of the hurdles you have overcome, and the life you have lived hand in hand. We need to be lifelong learners of our spouses—their habits, their favorite things, their pains and joys. We must be intentional in asking open-ended questions and following up with responses that show we are really listening and we truly care.

Accept each other's changes: you are both better together because of the hurdles you have overcome, and the life you have lived hand in hand.

One of my favorite memories with Ryan is a ten-hour road trip we took on our tenth anniversary. We did nothing but ask and answer questions about each other. (Obviously we were without the kiddos.) We learned so much about each other that trip, even after ten years of marriage. For example, I learned he hated putting other people's dirty dishes in the dishwasher—which made his hesitancy to do so make so much sense! Without intentionally seeking to know him better, that is a small thing that could have easily turned into a large wedge between us. It didn't, because I accepted the reasons he didn't like loading the dishwasher. He still handles others' dirty dishes from time to time; now it means that much more when he does.

How good are you at accepting your spouse? Maybe after a couple of years (or even decades) of tolerating a certain trait, it's starting to wear you down. Do you even know why your spouse has that particular habit, attitude, or behavior? Understanding our spouses better will lead to more acceptance. Also, expecting change will lead to a greater ability to accept your spouse when that change comes.

*Disclaimer: not all change is positive. Some life misfortunes can cause us to change in a major and negative way that requires major adjustment, such as when a spouse becomes ill or severely injured. Accepting change in this situation may need some professional help, and the help of family, friends, and your church.

There are certain behaviors that are unacceptable, including abuse (verbal, emotional, and physical), unfaithfulness, and illegal or highly risky activities, for example. If you are experiencing this in your marriage, accepting your spouse's destructive behavior isn't a hard and fast biblical rule. We urge you to seek professional help.

DIG DEEPER

Talk about it:

Take a moment and reminisce with your spouse about when you were first dating and then married. What were some traits that attracted you to each other? Be sure to include personality traits.

How have you seen a positive change in your spouse since then? Tell him or her how proud you are of the person they are becoming.

Take turns talking about a change you'd like to make and ask for accountability.

Pray about it:
Take turns praying out loud for each other. You can use the following prayer as a guide if you'd like; your prayer doesn't have to be limited to these words:

> *Dear God, Thank you so much for _____. Thank you for the person they have turned out to be. May we continue to grow together and to learn more and more about each other as the days and years pass. Give us the grace and compassion to accept each other for our faults and encourage each other to live our best life together for you. Amen.*

PRAY FOR AND WITH EACH OTHER

WEEK 6

||||||||||

VULNERABILITY

BEFORE YOU BEGIN
Take time to prepare your mind, your heart, and your space.
Be open to change; listen well and anticipate a positive experience.

START THE CONVERSATION

- What encouraged you this past week?
- What discouraged you this past week?
- What one thing can I do to help you in the week ahead?
- What are your prayer needs for the week ahead?

5-MINUTE READ-ALOUD

Ryan:

Have you ever seen the movie *A League of Their Own*? It's one of Jenny's favorite movies. The film takes place primarily in 1943, during World War II. Because of the war, the number of men's pro baseball teams dropped to just a handful. To keep baseball going, the first women's baseball league was created.

There is a famous scene in the movie where the head coach of the team, played by Tom Hanks, tells the women, "There is no crying in baseball."[6]

I have heard that line numerous times in sports. In fact, I have said it to my son when it comes to soccer. I grew up believing that you just need to "man up" and hide your emotions, especially in sports. However, this idea (especially for men) of hiding your emotions often spills over in every area of our lives—especially in marriage.

As the movie progressed, we watched this team of strangers become friends that, well, did a lot of crying together. They allowed themselves to become vulnerable, and as they did, they drew closer and became a better team—and they grew to love each other more than the game.

Do you struggle with being vulnerable? Maybe you have been hurt severely in a relationship and that has caused you to keep things close to the chest.

I believe that vulnerability is an essential part of having a healthy, vibrant relationship. Now, I am not saying you should allow your emotions to dictate your actions, but it is important to unpack and process your emotions in a healthy way. And your spouse should be the primary person on this earth for this kind of vulnerability.

Vulnerability is an essential part of having a healthy, vibrant marriage.

While we don't have enough time to explore this topic extensively, I want to point your attention to the vulnerability of Jesus. He exemplified what it looks like to be vulnerable in a healthy way. On his way to the cross (Matthew 26:36–39) he had a conversation with Peter, James, and John. In the Garden of Gethsemane, he told them, "My soul is very sorrowful and troubled… even to death." From there, he approached the Father in prayer three times asking for this cup, his death, to pass from him. However, Jesus asked that the will of God be done.

I would encourage you as a married couple to pay attention to the many times in which Jesus was vulnerable in his relationships. And take notice: this is not a sign of weakness, but rather a mark of strength.

DIG DEEPER

Talk about it:
- On a scale of 1 to 10, how vulnerable are you with your spouse?

- What causes you to withhold your feelings or vulnerabilities from your spouse? It is pride? Fear?
- In your weekly conversations this month, pay attention to when you might be holding back something that makes you feel vulnerable and, instead, share it. Be honest with your spouse about your struggle. Notice how this act of authenticity deepens your marriage.

PRAY FOR AND WITH EACH OTHER

WEEK 7

|||||||||

SACRIFICE

Take time to prepare your mind, your heart, and your space.
Be open to change; listen well and anticipate a positive experience.

START THE CONVERSATION
- What encouraged you this past week?
- What discouraged you this past week?
- What one thing can I do to help you in the week ahead?
- What are your prayer needs for the week ahead?

5-MINUTE READ-ALOUD

Jenny:

What pops in your mind when you hear the word *sacrifice*? Maybe you think of the sacrifices made by members of the military, emergency rescue, or law enforcement. Perhaps you have sacrificed a job to care for your family or sacrificed time with your family so that you can work to provide for them. There's a chance you recall a sacrifice that was made on your behalf. Why do we remember such sacrifices? Because of the very nature of the word. Sacrifice requires giving up something good for something greater, even if we don't personally benefit from it; we tend to remember, or recognize, the cost of sacrifice.

We see sacrifices being made all around us. In business or sports negotiations leaders may let go of a great opportunity or team member for something or someone even better. Volunteers give up precious time to help important causes or people in need. Donors sacrifice hard-earned money to help those less fortunate or support a church or ministry. Parents are always sacrificing for their children. Even the seemingly small sacrifices, like letting someone else choose where you eat, or giving up your parking spot, require an "others first" attitude. In the Bible, we learn about people bringing sacrificial offerings to God to show him their love, to atone for a sin they've committed, and to celebrate God's love and provision.

Sacrifice requires giving up something good for something greater.

When I think of sacrifice, the first thing that enters my mind is Christ's sacrifice on the cross to show God's never-ending love for his people. It cost everything, but was done out of a love so great that sacrifice was the only way to show that love. In fact, in John 15:13, Jesus told his disciples that sacrificing one's life is the greatest offering for love and friendship: *"Greater love has no one than this: to lay down one's life for one's friends."*

Part Three of *The Marriage Experience* is based on friendship because your spouse should also be your friend; ultimately, your *favorite* friend— your *best* friend. We should consider it an honor to sacrifice for our spouses out of love for them, but also out of love and reverence for the One who made the biggest sacrifice for us: God, through his Son, Jesus.

What does sacrifice in a marriage look like? When I think of sacrificing for my husband, I am reminded of *why* and *how* I make sacrifices in my marriage. It doesn't mean I begrudgingly give up what I want to eat for dinner to appease my spouse's appetite. It doesn't mean I forego that beach vacation my heart was set on, all the while keeping a mental score so, *next* year, *he* will make the sacrifice. It also doesn't mean that I make sacrifices to reward my husband's positive behavior, meaning that sacrifice only happens when it's deserved or earned. Sacrifice means I love my husband so much, regardless of the love he shows to me, that I am willing to give up my desires, what I want, to display that love. I do not keep score. I do not make sacrifices to keep him happy (although that is a nice outcome), nor to fill my "quota" so I will be seen as a "good wife," but to represent Christ's love in my marriage. I sacrifice because of love.

Many times, sacrifice hurts. As a parent, I cry sometimes thinking of God's sacrifice of his only Son. I can't even imagine the pain. He knew it would hurt, but he did it anyway. And guess what? We didn't deserve it then, and we don't now; but still his sacrifice was given to us freely. Likewise, I should make sacrifices for my husband, even during those times when I don't feel he deserves it, or when I know I am going to feel it, because that's the kind of sacrificial love that was shown to me on the cross. We are called to die to ourselves daily to follow Christ more closely. Sacrificing for my spouse is a beautiful way to show my love toward him *and* to God.

DIG DEEPER

Talk about it:
In what ways do you notice your spouse making sacrifices for you and your marriage? In what ways do you feel you sacrifice for your spouse and marriage? Remember to focus on each other only for this exercise, not children, other family, church, or anyone else.

Think about it:
How good are you at accepting a sacrifice from your spouse? Are you able to receive such a sacrifice with appreciation? Sometimes pride gets in the way when we receive love in any form, especially when someone is giving up something in order to show it. If your answer to this question is "not very well," I encourage you to push your pride aside the next time you see your spouse sacrificing something for you. Show appreciation and acceptance with love, allowing them to bless you.

PRAY FOR AND WITH EACH OTHER

WEEK 8

||||||||||

TRUST

BEFORE YOU BEGIN
Take time to prepare your mind, your heart, and your space.
Be open to change; listen well and anticipate a positive experience.

START THE CONVERSATION
- What encouraged you this past week?
- What discouraged you this past week?
- What one thing can I do to help you in the week ahead?
- What are your prayer needs for the week ahead?

5-MINUTE READ-ALOUD
Ryan:

I'll be honest; trust doesn't come easy for me. I will trust you *as long as* you don't let me down. I was the kicker for my high school football team, and in that position, I had to trust my teammates. I had to trust the holder to catch and position the ball quickly. I had to trust the linemen to protect me from being "roughed" by the opposing team. *As long as* they didn't let me down, I could trust them and do my part. *Without* trust, we could not perform in step. When my trust was shaken, my performance was also shaken.

I want to take you back to 2013 for a moment. If you were in church at that time, then it's likely that you heard or sang the song "Oceans (Where Feet May Fail)" by Hillsong United. This song (while probably being overplayed) has a lyric in the bridge that has stayed with me ever since the first listen. It says: "Spirit lead me where my trust is without borders."

Have you thought about trust in that way? So often, as Christians we place a box around our trust in God. We will trust him *as long as* we are financially stable. We will trust him *as long as* we stay right where we are. We will trust him *as long as* [fill in the blank]. This kind of "*as long as*" trust is *not* fully trusting God.

If we have issues with fully trusting God, who is the Creator of the universe, and if we have trouble fully trusting in Jesus, who was sinless and perfect, then how can we fully trust our spouses who are broken and fallen? Do you have an *as long as* trust with your spouse, or do you trust them fully?

Complete trust inside the marriage relationship is essential to walking in step with your spouse. And trust must be a two-way street. Husbands, you not only need to trust your wife and believe that she wants what is best for you, but you must also be trustworthy and live in such a way that she believes the best in you.

Trust inside the marriage relationship is essential to walking in step with your spouse.

It's possible (even likely) that you are reading this and trust has been broken inside your marriage relationship. And you may be asking, how can I regain trust with my spouse, or how can I ever trust my spouse again?

First off, I just want to say that if you are the one who broke the trust of your spouse, know that there is forgiveness available in Jesus. Maybe you haven't asked for forgiveness from God, from your spouse, or from yourself. I would encourage you to start there.

If you are the one that had your trust broken, then I would ask you to consider what forgiving your spouse would look like. Forgiveness does not equal forgetting, but it is the first step in the process that leads to trust.

DIG DEEPER

Talk about it:
- What is one area you can grow in trusting your spouse? Share with each other.
- If you struggle with trusting your spouse fully, why is that? What is one step you can take to removing a border in your trust?
- As a couple, what is one way in which you do not fully trust in God? Why?

PRAY FOR AND WITH EACH OTHER

Fidelity is not the only area in marriage where trust can be broken. If you are struggling with a broken trust within your marriage, we recommend two things:

- Read Lysa TerKeurst's book, *Forgiving What You Can't Forget.*
- Seek professional help from a qualified Christian marriage and family counselor.

WEEK 9

IIIIIIIIII

COMPASSION

BEFORE YOU BEGIN

Take time to prepare your mind, your heart, and your space.
Be open to change; listen well and anticipate a positive experience.

START THE CONVERSATION

- What encouraged you this past week?
- What discouraged you this past week?
- What one thing can I do to help you in the week ahead?
- What are your prayer needs for the week ahead?

5-MINUTE READ-ALOUD

Jenny:

Have you ever witnessed your spouse suffering, maybe from a physical hurt like something as serious as a heart attack or simple as a splinter? What about emotional suffering, like the loss of a friendship or the hurtful words of a family member? Perhaps you have been the source of your spouse's suffering. As humans living in a wicked world, we suffer in so many ways, and it probably didn't take long in your marriage before you saw your spouse suffer, and were given the opportunity to show some compassion or concern for their troubles. Early on in a marriage, when feelings are warm and fuzzy, it's relatively easy to show compassion. But, as the months and years go by, you might find compassion and sympathy more difficult to muster. Perhaps it's because you've responded to a particular hurt so many times before. Maybe your spouse seems difficult to please, or isn't prioritizing your relationship the way you'd like, and your compassion is tapped out.

Let's flip the switch. When you suffer, do you share those feelings with your spouse? Wives, do you give your burdens to your spouse so they can help you carry the load, or do you hold back, perhaps thinking they have enough on their plate? Husbands, do you hide your sufferings because you don't want to be vulnerable with your wife?

"Put on then, as God's chosen ones, holy and beloved, compassionate hearts."
Colossians 3:12 (ESV)

This was a charge the apostle Paul gave to the church at Colossae to show concern for those who are suffering. Who sees our spouses suffer more than we do? If you are like Ryan and me, then the answer is "no one." While I understand there are some occupations that require your colleagues to see a vulnerable side of you, perhaps one that you don't want to take home, I urge you to allow your spouse in on that part of you too. And spouses, when your husband or wife lets you in on their sufferings, I implore you to consider it a privilege, not an obligation. Take it seriously.

Showing compassion to your spouse is a privilege, not an obligation.

In our weekly chats, Ryan and I discuss challenges from the week prior, so I know I always have an outlet, a time we have already set aside, to share with him. That doesn't mean, however, that I have to wait until that designated time to let him in on what's going on. Sometimes I need to share that same day when he is home from work, or even right after that particular phone call or moment of struggle.

Have you ever said or thought, "Why should I share my hurts? He never listens anyway!" When I approach Ryan with something that hurt me, I will usually start with a phrase that allows him to prepare his heart and mind to listen. It goes something like this: "Can I talk to you about something that I've been thinking about?" or "I know this might sound silly, but..." Giving him a verbal cue before I talk about the blow I've experienced creates a sort of buffer, letting him know I am letting down a guard on my heart to say something a little out of line from our usual conversation. And you know what? It works!

We all have bad moments, days, weeks even, but we weren't meant to keep our burdens to ourselves. When we married, we were called to leave our parents and cleave to our spouses. Especially in a new relationship, we may be more inclined to vent to our close friends or even our parents before our significant others. We need to build that relational habit of taking those struggles to our spouses first. Sharing your struggles with your spouse is healthy; it actually shows them how much you love and trust them. And, you are also able to show how much you love them by listening to their struggles and having the compassion for them that Paul wrote about in his letter to the church at Colossae.

It's not easy to share our struggles. When you observe that your spouse is burdened, they may need some encouragement to open up. Whenever they are able to communicate their hurts with you, regardless of how inconvenient the timing may be or how many times this same hurt has come up, show compassion. Give them encouragement and a safe space to talk to you.

DIG DEEPER

Talk about it:
Do you feel safe sharing your hurts with your spouse? Do you receive compassion from them in those moments? Does your spouse feel compassion from you in the midst of their hurts?

Ask:
Take turns and ask each other if there is a hurt or burden they would like to share, and then listen for the answer. Many times when we share a hurt, we are not looking for an answer; we just need to be heard. Make it clear to your spouse what you need!

PRAY FOR AND WITH EACH OTHER

WEEK 10

||||||||||

ROMANCE

BEFORE YOU BEGIN
Take time to prepare your mind, your heart, and your space.
Be open to change; listen well and anticipate a positive experience.

START THE CONVERSATION
- What encouraged you this past week?
- What discouraged you this past week?
- What one thing can I do to help you in the week ahead?
- What are your prayer needs for the week ahead?

5-MINUTE READ-ALOUD
Ryan:

While the Bible doesn't really address dating, it has quite a lot to say when it comes to sex and love in the marriage relationship. From Genesis 2:24 where marriage is described as "two becoming one," to the unmistakably sensual verses in Proverbs 5:19–20 (take a moment to look that one up), we know that romance and intimacy should be a central part of marriage.

Unfortunately, romance and sex are often viewed as things that are mutually exclusive. For instance, I would say that Jenny focuses more on the romance side, where I focus more on the sex part of the equation. Jenny would like for me to woo her in exciting and mysterious ways that will lead to sex. However, I tend to think that sex will lead to romance.

So, who is right? I would suggest we both are right—and we both are wrong.

Romance and sex are intertwined. And it should never be up to just one person to initiate romance, or just up to one person to initiate sex. Let me say that again:

Romance and sex are intertwined. It should never be up to just one person to initiate either.

What are some next steps then? Well, let me offer up a few:

- Talk about your sex and romance life regularly. How are things going? What are your needs and expectations? What is obstructing healthy sex and romance in your marriage?
- Carve out a regular rhythm of dating. Jenny and I date each other every week even if it is just coffee and talking. You should get dating on your calendar *first*.
- Set up some overnight time alone and out of the house, especially if you have children or others living with you. Jenny and I have one night away scheduled for each quarter. I think having at least two a year would be a good place to start.

DIG DEEPER

Talk about it:
- While talking about these things may feel awkward at first, you must communicate openly. Is the frequency of your sex life in a good place?
- How often should you date? Who is in charge of planning the date? Should you go back and forth in planning?
- What does romance mean to you? Ask each other and really listen to your spouse's response.

PRAY FOR AND WITH EACH OTHER

WEEK 11

||||||||||

LOYALTY

BEFORE YOU BEGIN
Take time to prepare your mind, your heart, and your space.
Be open to change; listen well and anticipate a positive experience.

START THE CONVERSATION
- What encouraged you this past week?
- What discouraged you this past week?
- What one thing can I do to help you in the week ahead?
- What are your prayer needs for the week ahead?

5-MINUTE READ-ALOUD

Jenny:

Who or what are you loyal to? Your church? Your gym? Your team? Your face wash? I do most of the grocery shopping in our household, and Ryan isn't particular about a lot of things, but there are a few things he will not take a substitute for. Peanut butter is one of those things. Fortunately for me, he has chosen a widely known and held brand that I don't have trouble finding. In a word, he is loyal. Why? Because he knows the integrity of the product is incomparable and it hasn't failed him… yet. But what if, one day, that peanut butter is a little too oily, doesn't taste right, or is being sold at an exponentially inflated price? Would he remain loyal? Or would he seek to find a different brand that meets his peanut butter demands? What does loyalty require? Unwavering, constant support. I know that sounds silly when you're talking about peanut butter, so let's take a more relational approach.

Have you ever been abandoned by a friend when you needed them most? Have you been hurt by friends who talked badly about you behind your back? Loyalty is so important in friendship—but what does loyalty look like in marriage? To me, the obvious answer is fidelity. Ryan talked about faithfulness in Part Two, so let's start there: are you faithful to your spouse? Maybe the short answer is yes, but let's look a little deeper, because loyalty goes beyond faithfulness. Have you given your spouse constant and unwavering support? Still yes? Or did you have to think about that one a little harder? Have you stayed true to your commitment to love and cherish them in sickness and health, for richer or poorer, in the good times and the bad? Or have you turned to something or someone else that better meets your needs or is easier to be loyal to?

As Christ followers, the greatest example of loyalty we have is God. Even when we are faithless, when we doubt, when we choose the world over his Word, when idols creep in, he is faithful and loyal to us. Time and time again in the Old Testament, we see the Israelites grumble and complain, even threaten to go back to being oppressed when things didn't go the way they planned, or when they weren't happy with their circumstances. Did God leave? No. Did God find another group of people to love and provide for? No. Was God hurt? Undoubtedly so. He was and is a jealous God, yet even still…he was loyal to his people thousands of years ago—and he is loyal to you today. Like the Israelites, have you been grumbling and complaining about your spouse to others? Have you perhaps even threatened to leave because of your circumstances? If so, you have not been loyal.

So I ask again: who, or what, are you loyal to?

Are you loyal to your spouse when things aren't going the way you had hoped and even planned? Do you show unwavering support when your spouse is unhappy, or do you brush off their discontent? Do you listen when they are sad? Help when they are sick?

If you feel that your support of your spouse has been unreliable rather than constant, fickle instead of unwavering, perhaps it's time you renew your commitment. You don't have to wait for an anniversary or a grand moment. If something is nudging you right now to respond, don't wait. Let your spouse know what's on your heart. Ask for forgiveness for not being loyal to them in a constant or reliable way. Then, make a commitment to do better—and actually take action. Loyalty is a choice. What, or who, is feeding your disloyalty? What will you do about it, and when? Write it down on your calendar. Set an alarm on your phone. Do whatever it takes to move your decision to action. Psalm 85:10 says that love and faithfulness meet together. In this passage, we are reminded of God's love for his people based on his covenant, or promise, to them. With love comes loyalty. You, too, have made a promise.

Steadfast love and faithfulness meet; righteousness and peace kiss each other.
Psalm 85:10 (ESV)

If you feel that your support of your spouse has been unreliable rather than constant, fickle instead of unwavering, perhaps it's time you renew your commitment.

DIG DEEPER

Talk about it:
If you are feeling that you are not on the receiving end of such loyalty, let this be a safe space to lovingly say so. What or who have you felt your spouse put before you? Give them a chance to respond. This should never be a one-way conversation. The purpose of talking about loyalty isn't to make your spouse feel bad, but rather open up a conversation on the road to a healthier marriage.

PRAY FOR AND WITH EACH OTHER

WEEK 12

||||||||||

PRESENCE

BEFORE YOU BEGIN
Take time to prepare your mind, your heart, and your space.
Be open to change; listen well and anticipate a positive experience.

START THE CONVERSATION
- What encouraged you this past week?
- What discouraged you this past week?
- What one thing can I do to help you in the week ahead?
- What are your prayer needs for the week ahead?

5-MINUTE READ-ALOUD
Ryan:

You may have read the title to this week's conversation starter and thought, what is "presence"?

How many hours have you spent together with your spouse this week, perhaps at home or at a restaurant, while one or both of you have your attention fixed on a television screen or your phone? By contrast, how many minutes have you spent looking at each other, listening and responding, paying attention to each other? Don't worry; being present doesn't mean you can never have any down time or screen time. So what does it mean?

Well, we mean "being there" for your spouse. Showing up. Really listening, and truly being engaged.

I have a close friend, a pastor that I try to connect with on a regular basis. The purpose of our FaceTime calls is to catch up and see how ministry is going. This friend is a great listener. Do you want to know how I know this? He asks great questions. In fact, there are many times where I have to tell him to stop asking questions so I can hear about his life and how his church is doing.

Are you present for your spouse? Are you a good listener? Do you ask great questions?

Being present for your spouse means showing up, really listening, and truly being engaged.

One of my favorite podcasts is the *Carey Nieuwhof Leadership* podcast. In addition to providing great leadership material, the reason I like it so much is because Carey asks great questions. He is a great listener and is present for the people he interviews. In one episode, one of his guests made this observation: "Jesus asked three hundred and seven questions and answered only eight questions."

In the New Testament, we see that Jesus was a great listener and asked great questions. In James 1:19 we are told to be slow to speak and quick to listen.

If you want your marriage to grow, be a better listener to your spouse.

If you want your marriage to thrive, regularly ask questions of your spouse.

If you want to put the gospel on display in your marriage, be present for your spouse.

DIG DEEPER

Talk about it:
- When is the last time you asked your spouse an attentive question about themselves or something specific going on in their life? What was the question?
- How might you improve your listening skills in the context of your marriage?

- What is one area or topic where you can be present for your spouse by just listening without feeling the need to give advice?
- Conversations don't always have to be serious. Take some time to search for a relationship questionnaire online that will help you learn new things about each other. Set a time to walk through this with your spouse.

PRAY FOR AND WITH EACH OTHER

WEEK 13

||||||||||

CELEBRATION

BEFORE YOU BEGIN
Take time to prepare your mind, your heart, and your space.
Be open to change; listen well and anticipate a positive experience.

START THE CONVERSATION
- What encouraged you this past week?
- What discouraged you this past week?
- What one thing can I do to help you in the week ahead?
- What are your prayer needs for the week ahead?

5-MINUTE READ-ALOUD
You did it! By the end of this week, you will have completed the first three parts of *The Marriage Experience*—that's thirty-nine weeks of intentional investment in your marriage! You are poised to head into the future stronger and closer to each other and to God than ever before. You covered topics that may have opened old wounds or revealed some rough spots, or perhaps you polished up the most beautiful aspects of your marriage so that the world can more easily see God in your relationship. That's all part of the process, and all perfect!

Even if you still have a lot to work on, you are ready to look ahead into the future, which is the topic of the fourth and final part of *The Marriage Experience*. And, the *future* really is something to look forward to! But for now, even though we suggested you enjoy mini-celebrations at the end of each week's conversation, it's time again to celebrate in a more intentional way—and we have one more topic on friendship to talk about: your marriage and friendships with other people.

Your spouse comes before all other earthly relationships.

Most of us have friends outside our marriages, whether from work, the gym, our neighborhood, church, parents of our kids' friends, or we may even think of our own children as our friends. As important as some of those friendships are, we must protect our marriages from *all other relationships*. This does not mean that we do away with them, but it does mean we must never be deceitful with our spouse about those friends. We must guard ourselves from inappropriate relationships, and must never speak or act disrespectfully toward our spouse when we engage in those relationships. Sometimes, we do need to end or put a boundary between us and those friends who have a negative influence on us or our marriage.

Does this mean it's better not to have friends outside of our marriage? Not at all! Remember, your spouse can and should be your best and most important friend—not your only friend. How you nurture your other friendships should be defined within the context of your marriage, but here are some things to think and talk about: opposite sex relationships, using terms like "work spouse," talking negatively about your spouse or sensitive subjects regarding your spouse. We should have relationships outside of our marriages and the desire to do so is biblical. We were made for community. Healthy friendships are vital to our mental health and spiritual growth. But we also know that the devil is prowling around like a lion; he knows an easy way to get in between a couple is with other relationships. Remember, your spouse comes before all other earthly relationships.

This time, the object of your celebration should be *romance*. If you can combine romance with something fun that leaves you laughing, that's a perfect combination to celebrate and reflect on the friendship of your marriage. If you can initiate a group date with some healthy friends, even better!

Enjoy each other, and take a minute to read the intro to the final leg of your *Marriage Experience* journey. We're excited to join you next week!

PRAY FOR AND WITH EACH OTHER

PART FOUR//FUTURE

|||||||||||

OVER THE PAST SEVERAL months, you have heard from us individually on thirty-nine different topics, all designed to bring you to this moment. You have heard our separate voices and perspectives, as different as you and your spouse are from each other, yet both leading you on a very intentional path and preparing you for these next thirteen weeks.

Our editor noticed something interesting in these last few topics, and you also may notice it as you enjoy each five-minute read-aloud: our voices are starting to merge. We are sounding more and more like each other. Each message has always been carefully planned but the content developed independent of each other. But now, without intention, without pre-planning, our specific points are very much in sync, just like one of those couples who can finish each other's sentences.

Where the first three parts of this series focused on general principles, examining current and past experiences, and short-term immediate goals, these last few weeks are more long-term. You will likely laugh, and probably shed tears of joy. You may spend a little extra time pondering some questions together, and realize as you go how much progress you have already made.

So, buckle up, roll down the windows, and enjoy the journey as the final part of *The Marriage Experience* unfolds.

Let's start the conversation—Part Four!

Ryan and Jenny

WEEK 1

||||||||||

PURPOSE

Take time to prepare your mind, your heart, and your space.
Be open to change; listen well and anticipate a positive experience.

START THE CONVERSATION
- What encouraged you this past week?
- What discouraged you this past week?
- What one thing can I do to help you in the week ahead?
- What are your prayer needs for the week ahead?

5-MINUTE READ-ALOUD

Ryan:

What is the purpose of marriage?

In the introduction to Part One of *The Marriage Experience* we talked about this question. We have talked about a lot of topics since then, all of them designed to help you as a couple fulfill this purpose. Now, as we begin our final series of topics, it's important that we clarify a few things here. I want to distinguish the difference between the purpose of marriage and the reasons we get married.

I like to collect shoes. I like to buy and sell shoes. The reason I buy most of my shoes is to sell them. I enjoy knowing what shoes are going to be popular. I like to know what shoes will sell out and become rare shoes. Those are reasons why I have a collection of shoes. However, shoes were created to be worn. Their purpose is to protect our feet. Do you see the difference?

There are many reasons to get married, both worldly and biblical. Let me list a few common reasons people have gotten married: They thought their spouse looked really good! They were in love and thought that was the next step. They wanted to have sex and not feel bad about it. They wanted to have some financial security. Perhaps they wanted to start a family. The Bible gives some reasons to get married. For example, Proverbs 18:22 says that "he who finds a wife finds a good thing and obtains favor from the LORD." In 1 Corinthians 7:9 we read that if one "cannot exercise self-control, they should marry. For it is better to marry than to burn with passion." These are all reasons to get married, and there are many, many more—but none of these reasons express the purpose of marriage.

It's likely you came into marriage with some preconceived notions as to the purpose of marriage. You may have thought the purpose of marriage is to be loved by someone. You may have thought the purpose of marriage is to have babies, or to prove your commitment to each other. And while those are all great things, they are reasons for marriage—not the purpose of marriage.

So then, I ask again, what is the purpose of marriage?

In Ephesians chapter 5, the apostle Paul explained the glorious purpose of marriage. After unpacking several things about marriage, like submission and love, he wrote this:

> Therefore a man shall leave his father and mother and hold fast to his wife, and the two shall become one flesh. This mystery is profound, and I am saying that it refers to Christ and the church.

And there you have it.

The purpose of marriage is to reflect the relationship that Jesus Christ has with the church.

When Jenny and I got married, we did not understand this. I think I got married for a lot of great reasons, and I know I loved Jesus when making my vows to my wife, but I really did not yet understand that there was a purpose in our marriage that went far beyond the two of us.

Here is the thing: when you understand the purpose of marriage, it will change everything in your life.

- Marriage is meant to be Jesus-centered.
- Marriage is meant to be gospel-centered.
- Marriage is meant to be full of grace and sacrifice.

Are these things at the center of your marriage?

When you understand the purpose of marriage, it will change everything in your life.

DIG DEEPER

Talk about it:
- What are some of the reasons you got married?
- In what ways do you believe you are putting the gospel (Jesus) on display in your marriage?
- If your marriage does not consistently display the gospel, why not? What are you displaying instead of Jesus?
- What is one small step you can take as a couple to better exemplify Christ and the church in your marriage?

PRAY FOR AND WITH EACH OTHER

WEEK 2

||||||||||

MISSION

BEFORE YOU BEGIN

Take time to prepare your mind, your heart, and your space.
Be open to change; listen well and anticipate a positive experience.

START THE CONVERSATION

- What encouraged you this past week?
- What discouraged you this past week?
- What one thing can I do to help you in the week ahead?
- What are your prayer needs for the week ahead?

5-MINUTE READ-ALOUD

Jenny:

One holiday season I signed up to bring single-serving pies to the school where our daughter attended. I understood the assignment well enough: go to the store, find the individually boxed pies, buy the committed amount of those pies, and deliver them. However, when I got to the store, there were no single-serving pies anywhere. Not in the bakery nor down the packaged goods aisle. When I asked the person behind the counter about them, he simply replied, "We didn't get any in our last shipment and I don't know when we will." All of a sudden, a seemingly simple task became a challenge. But I couldn't quit. Someone was depending on my commitment. I went to a few other stores in search of these pies. In the meantime, I contemplated buying pie bites or other small pastries in their place, but I knew doing so would have diminished the integrity of the assignment. I had to go on a mission.

Have you ever thought of your mission in marriage? Many of us begin our commitment to each other in a way similar to how I approached the pie assignment: we think we know what it means to get married, and we think we understand the assignment. We may think the assignment is to have a ceremony, say some things in front of people, exchange rings, have a party and move in together, where we will live the rest of our lives. But God desires more for our marriage—a lot more.

As Ryan said last week, every theme we've covered up to now has been leading to these last critical topics. Part Three of *The Marriage Experience* focused entirely on a critical part of our mission in marriage: friendship. God desires us to be friends, best friends even, in our marriage. In his book *The Meaning of Marriage*, Tim Keller states that real Christian friendship requires spiritual constancy, spiritual transparency, with a "deep oneness that develops as two people journey together toward the same destination, helping one other through the dangers and challenges along the way."[7] It will take this kind of friendship, and no less, to complete your mission in marriage.

So, what should the mission of your marriage be? Is there a distinction between the purpose of marriage and your mission within your own marriage?

My purpose as one of my daughter's classroom parents was to support the teacher and students of that one class in order to promote a healthy learning environment. My mission on that particular holiday was to provide single-serving pies.

Our purpose in marriage is to present the gospel and be an example of Jesus' relationship with the church. Our mission in our marriage is more specific. It defines what our purpose looks like, how it plays out. When people look at your marriage, what do they see? Two people putting the needs of the other in front of his or her own? People dying to themselves to lift the other up? Two people selflessly giving to each other?

A mission is an assignment. Do you understand your assignment in marriage? One way to get focused on your mission in marriage together is to write a mission statement. I've seen these many places, from businesses to classrooms and even family mission statements. Mission statements include three things: purpose, values, and goals. We just heard what the purpose of marriage is: to exemplify the gospel through our relationship and glorify God. What would that look like in your marriage? How might you specifically live out that purpose?

What is your marriage mission statement?

One way to get focused on your mission in marriage together is to write a mission statement.

I was able to find the individual pies. But it took knowing exactly what the assignment was, relentless pursuit of the target, and the unwavering decision not to accept a substitute.

DIG DEEPER

Do it:

Take the rest of your time together discussing some values and goals for your marriage to create a marriage mission statement of your own. This might take some thought and/or change in behavior. The purpose of a mission statement is to be a guardrail and guide for your marriage. When faced with a decision, you can use the statement to determine whether or not it makes sense for your marriage. When you feel like giving up or changing the assignment to fit what you think you're able to do, it will serve as a reminder.

Get creative:

Write your marriage mission statement in a place where it is visible to both of you. You could add a photo or create your own graphic on a free app or freehand if you are capable! Print it out and put it in a nice frame or hang it on your bathroom mirror or fridge so it can be a daily reminder.

PRAY FOR AND WITH EACH OTHER

WEEK 3

|||||||||

RHYTHM

BEFORE YOU BEGIN

Take time to prepare your mind, your heart, and your space.
Be open to change; listen well and anticipate a positive experience.

START THE CONVERSATION

- What encouraged you this past week?
- What discouraged you this past week?
- What one thing can I do to help you in the week ahead?
- What are your prayer needs for the week ahead?

5-MINUTE READ-ALOUD

Ryan:

When I first started in ministry, I thought that balance was essential to a thriving youth ministry. I thought I needed to have equal parts teaching, worship, fun, small groups, events, and the list would go on and on. I thought my calendar needed to be balanced as well. I would spend the perfect amount of time at work, and the perfect amount of time with family. After about a year of trying to achieve balance, I realized that balance wasn't attainable.

Has your marriage ever been in balance? Many husbands and wives struggle with the thought that their lives need balance, that we must give a certain amount of time to our church, spouse, kids, work, family, sports, and the list goes on.

What if achieving balance is a myth? What if, instead of balance, the goal was to find a healthy rhythm?

In Ecclesiastes 3:1–8, Solomon wrote that there is a time, or a season, for so many things in life. Understanding this truth is crucial to developing and sustaining a godly marriage. While it sounds optimal to have the scales of life perfectly balanced in your marriage, the key to a God-honoring and healthy marriage is to have an intentional rhythm.

Rhythm is a repeated pattern. In marriage, rhythm includes the regular things you keep sacred and give priority to—not just activities, but behaviors and attitudes. Even when the pace of life speeds up, the rhythm keeps you centered until it slows again. If you have established a strong rhythm, outside interruptions or the chaos of life will be less likely to throw you off. Rather than allowing other people or outside interests to set your rhythm for you and your spouse, you must determine your own rhythm.

And that rhythm will change throughout your marriage. That rhythm will look different before kids, and it will be adjusted when you are empty nesters. The rhythm will change when you have young children, and your marriage will look different again when you have teenagers in the home.

The key to a God-honoring and healthy marriage is to have an intentional rhythm.

The key to keeping in rhythm with your spouse is intentional communication, and just by having this weekly devotion time together you are taking an important step. So rather than viewing your marriage as scales that need to be balanced, might I suggest you think of your marriage as a journey. As you journey down that road, you will veer off to the left or to the right. But along the road you can set up guardrails that will help you come back to center. Jenny suggested last week that your marriage mission statement can be thought of as a guardrail, a safety fence to keep your marriage from running off the road. Establishing your rhythm is also like putting up those guardrails.

As you travel through this year together, seek clarity on the rhythm of your marriage. Make a covenant to keep those rhythmic elements that draw you ever closer to Jesus and to each other.

DIG DEEPER

Talk about it:
- What season of life are you in right now? How has this season affected the rhythm of your marriage?
- In what ways do you feel like your spouse needs to balance the scales in your marriage? If this feeling is negatively affecting your marriage, what about your mindset needs to shift?
- What are one or two essential rhythms that you need to implement in your marriage?

PRAY FOR AND WITH EACH OTHER

WEEK 4

||||||||||

COMMITMENT

BEFORE YOU BEGIN
Take time to prepare your mind, your heart, and your space.
Be open to change; listen well and anticipate a positive experience.

START THE CONVERSATION
- What encouraged you this past week?
- What discouraged you this past week?
- What one thing can I do to help you in the week ahead?
- What are your prayer needs for the week ahead?

5-MINUTE READ-ALOUD
Jenny:

When researching the top reasons people seek divorce, a main theme I found was a lack of commitment. I don't know about you, but to me that seems over simplified. A "lack of commitment" is almost the definition of divorce. It can't be that simple, can it? The more I study marriage, the more like rocket science it can seem—complicated, and hard. The news that a lack of commitment is a warning sign of a possible breakdown in the marriage seems like a no-brainer. Surely we can avoid that. Yet, the truth that many husbands and wives are not fully committed to each other plagues marriage after marriage, year after year.

When we commit to our spouses on our wedding day, what exactly are we committing to? The traditional wedding vows say something along the lines of, "I take you to have and to hold for better or worse, richer or poorer, in sickness and in health, to love and cherish all the days of our life." I remember saying those words, or something very similar at the ripe old age of twenty. I don't think I really understood what that commitment consisted of at the time. Ryan mentioned the same feeling in Week One, saying,

> When Jenny and I got married, we did not understand this. I think I got married for a lot of great reasons, and I know I loved Jesus when making my vows to my wife, but I really did not yet understand that there was a purpose in our marriage that went far beyond the two of us.

Even after a long engagement, we hadn't had very many, if any, "bad" days. We were generally in good shape, and the money didn't matter much, because we were broke! In layman's terms, those vows mean: "I want you to be mine, and I will be yours, every single day regardless of good days or bad days, how much money we have or how healthy we are. Every day I will love you, protect you, and care for you for as long as I am alive." That is quite a commitment. It's no wonder things fall apart when a lack of commitment is displayed in a marriage, when we are really saying, "I want you to be mine, and I will be yours, until it's just not working for me anymore."

When Jesus was calling his disciples to him, asking them to stop what they were doing and follow him, their response was a commitment to his work and plans for God's kingdom. It was not a spur-of-the-moment decision. They had spent time with him and made a mental, conscious decision to redirect their daily efforts toward him. They spent the rest of their lives devoting their time, energy, their whole selves to the gospel. Were they perfect at following him? No! They had to constantly be reminded of why they made their commitment and what that meant for them. Did Jesus send them away the first, second, or twentieth time they slacked on their commitment to him? No again. He gave them grace. He loved them. He was their friend, and he gave them another chance.

Just like us. We mess up with God daily. Our affections for him wane at times and we have to be reminded of how we are called to love him in our thoughts and actions. God extends grace to us; when we mess up, he doesn't kick us out or abandon us, ever. He is committed to us. When we extend that kind of grace to our spouse, we are fulfilling the very purpose of our marriage: to put the gospel on display.

Where are you in your commitment to each other? Do you remember the vows you promised on your wedding day? I'm certain you have had days when you upheld your promise beautifully. Undoubtedly, you have had days your commitment has not measured up to your promise all that time ago. Maybe it's time we stop and think about that promise. Realign with each other. Take inventory on the ways we have selfishly used our time and energy or neglected to devote those things to our spouse and the marriage.

> **When we extend grace to our spouse, we are fulfilling the very purpose of our marriage: to put the gospel on display.**

DIG DEEPER

Write it:
Take a few moments to write or rewrite a set of vows to each other. You can use the traditional vows above to help you get started or come up with them all on your own.

Say it:
Take turns speaking your vows aloud to each other. Keep in mind this can be a vulnerable, emotional activity, so be sensitive to each other's hesitancy or awkwardness.

Set it:
Put these vows in a place where you can be reminded of them often, perhaps on your mirror or fridge, as a bookmark, or in your car. Seeing these will be a reminder of your commitment to your friendship and your marriage.

PRAY FOR AND WITH EACH OTHER

WEEK 5

¦¦¦¦¦¦¦¦

INVESTMENT

BEFORE YOU BEGIN
Take time to prepare your mind, your heart, and your space.
Be open to change; listen well and anticipate a positive experience.

START THE CONVERSATION
- What encouraged you this past week?
- What discouraged you this past week?
- What one thing can I do to help you in the week ahead?
- What are your prayer needs for the week ahead?

5-MINUTE READ-ALOUD

Ryan:

I mentioned earlier that I like to buy and sell sneakers. When I first started collecting, I would spend money on shoes primarily just to wear them. However, around a decade ago, I started to invest in sneakers. I started buying sneakers with the intention of getting a return on my money. Those sneakers, my investment sneakers, I protect carefully.

Have you ever thought about the difference between spending and investing? As a child, spending is all you do if you have money. You buy toys, candy, video games, etc. Most of those items end up being worn out, broken, consumed, or given to the thrift store. What little value they may have had to begin with quickly disappears. But if you are fortunate, as you mature, you may begin to invest your money in hopes you will get a return on that investment.

The Bible is clear that Christians should have an investment mindset. Second Corinthians 9:6 says, "Whoever sows sparingly will also reap sparingly, and whoever sows bountifully will also reap bountifully."

You are probably familiar with this verse. In context, the apostle Paul was talking about giving. However, this sowing principle applies to marriage as well.

When it comes to your marriage, you should have an investment mindset.

Do you invest in your marriage?

Here are a few things to consider when answering this question. First of all, do you give your spouse the firstfruits of your time, or the leftovers? Are you spending your time on things that lose value or perhaps even eat away at your extremely valuable marriage, or are you investing your time in each other? If you give each other the firstfruits, then this means you are putting dates on the calendar first. You are putting vacations or overnight stays on the calendar first. Spending is often impulsive. Investing takes forethought.

Secondly, is the time you have with your spouse invested in such a way that yields dividends in the future? Now hear this before I get too far into this subject: Spending time with your spouse without a lot of conversation involved is not a bad thing. You can relax, watch TV, and do many other things with your spouse, and they can be good and right. However, are you also intentionally having conversations with your spouse that help to strengthen your marriage? If so, then you are investing in your marriage.

And finally, what are you willing to sacrifice for your marriage? To invest in something, that means you have to say no to other things. You need to allocate resources (time, energy, money, etc.) in order to invest in your marriage.

DIG DEEPER

Talk about it:
- In what ways do you spend time with your spouse?
- In what ways do you invest in your spouse?
- What is one thing you can say no to in order to invest more in your marriage?

Do it:
Schedule an overnight stay on your calendar for two months from now. By then, you will have completed Part Four of *The Marriage Experience*, and will have something special to look forward to.

PRAY FOR AND WITH EACH OTHER

WEEK 6

||||||||||

PLAY

BEFORE YOU BEGIN
Take time to prepare your mind, your heart, and your space.
Be open to change; listen well and anticipate a positive experience.

START THE CONVERSATION
- What encouraged you this past week?
- What discouraged you this past week?
- What one thing can I do to help you in the week ahead?
- What are your prayer needs for the week ahead?

5-MINUTE READ-ALOUD
Jenny:

"All work and no play makes Jack and Jill a dull couple." I know that is a "play" off of an old saying (pun completely intended), but it's true! Ryan and I met when we were kids, so play was a natural part of our relationship. We got married in college, and didn't have children for the first seven years of our marriage. Play looked like going to the park, singing together, going for long drives and listening to music, having picnics in the park, carving pumpkins at Halloween, and dressing up in old costumes. However, as we have grown up together and had to do more "adulting" (more like a-"dull"-ting), play has, in many seasons, taken a back seat to all of the other responsibilities we've taken on, like full time jobs, taking care of a home and yard, scheduling appointments, rearing children, feeding a family, more appointments, the list goes on and on. It's no wonder there is far less time for play.

The time spent "adulting" is only one reason why play suffers in our relationships as we get older. In the past few years, play has become scarce for me, partly because I grew up, became a changed person, and some of the playing I did when I was younger just doesn't sound appealing to me anymore. Sure, I do playful things now to entertain and make memories with our children. But we have had to make more of an effort at playing together as a couple.

Early on in our marriage, I gave Ryan one of the most heartfelt gifts he has ever received from me. (In case you have forgotten, I am not very sentimental, so this gift was pure gold.) I gave him a can with twelve Popsicle sticks in it. On each Popsicle stick, I had written a date idea. The premise of the gift was that, once a month, we would draw a stick and find time to do that date idea. Creating our date sticks back then was simple and easy enough, but if I were to make that gift again, the ideas would mostly be different. In fact, I might find it difficult to come up with twelve things that I would even consider "play." Sometimes I ask myself, "Do I even know what play means to me right now?"

Two things to consider: When discussing what play looks like in your marriage, be sure to talk about anything that makes you feel uncomfortable or convicted. This, too, can change over time as you mature, or grow closer in your relationship to Christ. Perhaps one of you is now convicted about the types of movies you watch or places you frequent for entertainment (or perhaps always were but never knew how to bring it up). By now, you should feel comfortable discussing these with your spouse, knowing you will be met with compassion and understanding, so be sure to speak up.

Also, the play I'm referring to here is within the context of marriage. I'm all about a girls' or guys' night out, but you should prioritize play with your spouse. If you find your schedule includes more hang time with friends than with your spouse, you are sending the message to everyone that your spouse is not your priority, which is unhealthy for your marriage, and does not reflect the relationship Jesus has with the church—the ultimate purpose of your marriage.

Play, as natural as it seems, becomes more unnatural the older we get and the more involved our lives become. Ryan and I have had to be more intentional at finding the time to play, and also consider how play has changed for us. We also have had to push each other to be more playful. Why? Because life is hard and, many times, draining. It's easy just to sit on the couch after a long work day or week and rest. Don't get me wrong—rest is good, biblical even. But we can't spend so much time resting that we lose time to play.

At times, resting and playing can even be one and the same. It's important to take time to define play within your marriage. To me, play in our marriage is anything that makes me laugh or gets me out of "mom mode." Ryan succinctly defines play as "the opposite of work." With those definitions, play doesn't have to always mean some grand gesture. These days, play in our marriage looks like coffee dates, board games, funny shows (and some serious ones), reading a good book together, even silly things we might say to each other, random kitchen dancing, or faces we make to each other.

It's important to note that play within marriage should mostly reflect that which is play to both of you. It's great to serve our spouse with play that reflects their desires, but it shouldn't always be so. And if you can't find something the both of you consider play, take that as a challenge to get out there and try new things together. Cooking classes, a new sport, hobby, or skill are just a few ideas. Keep trying until you find something you both love. The bottom line is that we must take the time to incorporate play into our marriages so we don't become a-"dull"-ts, like our friends Jack and Jill.

Play within marriage should mostly reflect that which is play to both of you.

Do you play together in your marriage?

DIG DEEPER

Define it:
Take a moment to define "play" in your marriage. Tell each other what ideas you have for play in your marriage, what you would think is fun,

different, or interesting. Remember not to be judgmental or scoff at any suggestions. If something doesn't seem like play to you, kindly tell your spouse that and be receptive and sensitive if your spouse shares that your idea of play isn't reciprocated. Hopefully at this point you have created a safe space around these conversations that you can share freely and honestly.

Talk about it:
Do you feel like you get sufficient "play" time together, or would you prefer more? Do you typically spend time playing together, or is most of your playtime alone or with people other than your spouse? Get on the same page about how well you are doing in this area, and make a decision right now to incorporate more play into your marriage by scheduling time to go do something fun (maybe something you named above)! Already feel successful in this area? Give each other a hearty high five and play a game to see who can make the other laugh the quickest.

PRAY FOR AND WITH EACH OTHER

WEEK 7

||||||||||

HOPE

BEFORE YOU BEGIN

Take time to prepare your mind, your heart, and your space.
Be open to change; listen well and anticipate a positive experience.

START THE CONVERSATION

- What encouraged you this past week?
- What discouraged you this past week?
- What one thing can I do to help you in the week ahead?
- What are your prayer needs for the week ahead?

5-MINUTE READ-ALOUD

Ryan:

When you hear the word *hope*, what do you think about? Maybe for you it is simply wishful thinking. You may say something like, "I *hope* I win the lottery." Or maybe, hope to you is the desires of your heart. You may say something like, "I *hope* my favorite sports team wins the championship."

Oftentimes, when we think of hope, we view it through the lens of chance.

However, as we look at a biblical hope, we know that it is so much more than that. In 1 Peter 1:3–5, we read this:

> Blessed be the God and Father of our Lord Jesus Christ! According
> to his great mercy, he has caused us to be born again to a living

hope through the resurrection of Jesus Christ from the dead, to an inheritance that is imperishable, undefiled, and unfading, kept in heaven for you, who by God's power are being guarded through faith for a salvation ready to be revealed in the last time.

Without completely unpacking this passage, I want to draw your attention to the word "hope" in verse 3. This verse tells us that when we are in Christ, when we have a relationship with Jesus, that we have been made new (or born again) and that we receive an inheritance that cannot be tarnished.

You see, not only is hope, in view of Jesus, not left up to chance, but it is also guaranteed. With this perspective in mind, what should hope look like in marriage? And specifically, what does hope look like in your marriage?

If your spouse has a relationship with God through Jesus Christ, do you view them as someone who has eternal hope and has received an inheritance from God? If so, then this should be the framework through which you view the future of your marriage. For example:

- Rather than blaming your husband for his shortcomings, you hope in the future that he will continue to grow in Jesus.
- Rather than seeking to control your wife, you see her as an image-bearer of the King, and you place your hope in the God who gives grace to the humble.
- Rather than finding security in your marriage through money, possessions, status, approval, or acceptance, you find your security in the unchangeable hope you have in Jesus Christ.
- Rather than seeing a future within your marriage as hopeless, you see it the way Jesus does: full of hope, not left up to chance, but guaranteed.*

Viewing your spouse as someone who has eternal hope and has received an inheritance from God should be the framework through which you view the future of your marriage.

Do you see your marriage as full of hope?

One of my favorite worship songs is by River Valley Worship, and it is called "Hope Has a Name."[8] In the chorus we are reminded time and time again that "hope has a name, His name is Jesus."

DIG DEEPER

Talk about it:
- In your marriage, if you are truly honest, what do you place your hope in?
- Maybe you have viewed hope through the lens of the world rather than through the Bible. If this is you, how will this new perspective change your outlook on hope in your marriage?
- What is one thing you are hoping for in your marriage?

(If you struggled with this idea of eternal hope, you are not alone. In the back of this book is a short chapter called "Inheritance," written just for you.)

PRAY FOR AND WITH EACH OTHER

As you read this week about hope, do you find that you do in fact feel hopeless about your marriage? Right now is the time to seek professional help. Do not delay. Find a marriage and family counselor who will respect and understand your faith. Go together; go separately. But go. Two weeks ago I spoke about investing in your marriage. Seeing a counselor may require some sacrifice, may cost some money, and will not be a quick fix, but is the most important investment couples can make for those who need it.

WEEK 8

iiiiiiii

DREAMS

BEFORE YOU BEGIN
Take time to prepare your mind, your heart, and your space.
Be open to change; listen well and anticipate a positive experience.

START THE CONVERSATION
- What encouraged you this past week?
- What discouraged you this past week?
- What one thing can I do to help you in the week ahead?
- What are your prayer needs for the week ahead?

5-MINUTE READ-ALOUD

Jenny:

When is the last time you had a dream? I'm not talking about the kind where you are running from a bear and it somehow enters your home without tearing down a door and all of a sudden you're hiding for your life. (That was pretty specific, wasn't it?) I'm referring to the kind of dream that takes your breath away when you think about it. The kind of dream that requires work, passion, time, energy—a beautiful reward for all of those things. Have you ever dreamed together with your spouse? More than planning for family vacation (although that might be part of a dream), more than preparing for the holidays, dreaming with your spouse is putting two minds together to think of a goal that includes both of your passions, desires, and hopes for God's will through it all.

Ryan and I began really dreaming with each other about three years ago. Keep in mind, we had been married for fourteen years and hadn't once dreamed past how we would spend a week in the summer, or whether or not we were ready for a mortgage (again, home ownership could very well be a part of your dream). Both of us had gone back to school to earn a master's degree, yet even in that, we weren't dreaming together. We sat down one evening with a notebook and pen and began thinking about what we wanted from our life together. How did we want our future to look? What passions did we share? How was God moving us toward each other? Considering our gifts and where we were physically, what had God already given us that we could use for him, to help others?

As we dreamed—of retirement, of our kids' futures, of working together—we landed somewhere near and dear to our hearts, and now, hopefully, to yours. We dreamed of creating a resource to support and encourage married couples, just like you, to put the gospel on display in your marriage, to laugh with each other, to learn about each other, to fight for each other, to model a messy yet beautiful marriage filled with grace for the next generation in your home. That dream began as an online resource (themarriageexperience.com), continued as a book, shifted to a download, and finally became the start of a beautiful journey and ministry, a dream come true that is still evolving and growing beyond our imaginations.

And you want to know what? Even if it hadn't come true, God is still good and our dreaming was too. Envisioning a future that includes your spouse is one of the best gifts you can give them, a wonderful expression of the living hope Ryan spoke about last week. It's about the journey you take together, the road trip we have both been talking to you about.

After the couple of years we all had during the pandemic, and now as the world feels more and more unstable, it might be hard to dream about anything. No one could have predicted how the virus might have derailed any hint of a dream Ryan and I had, but God still did mighty things—and it's not too late for your dreams together. The plans might shift, but the end result can still be the same.

**Envisioning a future that includes your spouse
is one of the best gifts you can give them.**

As Christians, we know that we can't predict the future, but we know who holds it. We know each day is a gift, but not a guarantee. I know there are some people out there who don't ever allow themselves to dream because there is no guarantee their plans will actually happen, no matter how hard they work. I would still implore you to dream and trust God in the steps.

DIG DEEPER

Talk about it:
When is the last time you dreamed together, if ever? Take several minutes and talk about your biggest dreams. Think about how you would like the next five or ten years to look. If you don't have time for an extended conversation now, plan a time to continue your dream talk. Think about the gifts God has given you to steward. How can you use those gifts for God? Can you use them together? How are you serving with each other? What steps would you need to take this month, quarter, or year to get you closer to that big dream? What sacrifices are you willing to make now and over the next few years to get there? Pray about it: Bring your dream to God. Ask him for direction, wisdom, guidance, and unity as you journey this road together.

PRAY FOR AND WITH EACH OTHER

WEEK 9

||||||||||

PERSEVERANCE

BEFORE YOU BEGIN
Take time to prepare your mind, your heart, and your space.
Be open to change; listen well and anticipate a positive experience.

START THE CONVERSATION
- What encouraged you this past week?
- What discouraged you this past week?
- What one thing can I do to help you in the week ahead?
- What are your prayer needs for the week ahead?

5-MINUTE READ-ALOUD

Ryan:

Have you ever taken a stress test for your heart? Have you ever even heard of a stress test? Your doctor might give you a stress test to find out if you have heart issues. The test determines how much stress can be put on the heart before abnormal rhythms start to occur. The greater amount of pain and suffering your heart can take, the stronger and healthier your heart.

In Romans 5:3–4 we read this: We rejoice in our sufferings, knowing that suffering produces endurance, and endurance produces character, and character produces hope.

Now, in the New International Version of the Bible, the word for endurance is perseverance—they are synonyms. But did you notice how verse 3 starts? It says to rejoice in your suffering. Why? Because suffering produces perseverance.

Just like a physical stress test, I believe that we have relational stress tests. And some of the biggest relational stress tests come in our marriages. Heart stress tests don't cause problems with your heart; they *reveal* them. The same is true for a relational stress test in your marriage. The stresses we endure as a couple don't create our problems, but they do reveal them.

With these things in mind, how do you view suffering in your marriage? This verse teaches us to rejoice in our sufferings, so that we can grow in perseverance. Rejoicing in painful circumstances is a choice we make, a deliberate act, rather than our natural reaction to pain. Think about a long-distance runner. If they put themselves through more training (more pain), they are able to run longer distances because their endurance, or perseverance, has increased.

The stresses we endure as a couple don't create our problems, but they do reveal them.

And here is the really cool thing about this passage in Romans. When you rejoice in your suffering, then you grow in perseverance. That, in turn, strengthens your character, or in this context, strengthens your marriage, and from that you grow in your hope, a topic we discussed just a couple of weeks ago. Are you beginning to see how each of these final thirteen weeks are connected?

In the context of marriage, the way you deal with suffering reveals a lot about your heart. It reveals a lot about where you put your trust. In your marriage, if you fully trust in Jesus, then you can honestly rejoice in your suffering, because you know in your heart that every trial in your marriage will produce perseverance. And from that perseverance, the character of your marriage will grow, part of the process of marital sanctification. This growth is what helps us to fulfill our marriage mission of reflecting Jesus to a broken world—not a perfect marriage, but a marriage that is growing. Every process of sanctification, or growth, in your marriage reflects the gospel to others and points you back to hope. And, as we've said before, hope has a name, and his name is Jesus.

DIG DEEPER

Talk about it:

- As married couples we have all gone through stresses together. Have you been able to rejoice together in your suffering? Why or why not?
- What has been (or is) the greatest relational stress test in your marriage? Can you see where that situation is producing perseverance in your marriage? Why or why not?

PRAY FOR AND WITH EACH OTHER

WEEK 10

||||||||||

GROWTH

BEFORE YOU BEGIN
Take time to prepare your mind, your heart, and your space.
Be open to change; listen well and anticipate a positive experience.

START THE CONVERSATION
- What encouraged you this past week?
- What discouraged you this past week?
- What one thing can I do to help you in the week ahead?
- What are your prayer needs for the week ahead?

5-MINUTE READ-ALOUD
Jenny:

In last week's topic, Ryan talked about how our response to suffering leads to perseverance in our marriage, which leads to growth in the character of our marriage. This week we are going to talk very practically about intentional growth in our marriage. Before we begin, take a moment to discuss the following questions:

- Does change mean growth, and if so, when?
- Does growth mean change, and if so, when?

I am reminded in my marriage of something I read in Tim and Kathy Keller's *The Meaning of Marriage*[9]: we all change. In fact, he goes on to say that many of us change many times as we grow older, gain experience, and mature in certain situations, or are impacted negatively by other circumstances. I have also said that, especially in our relationship with our spouse, we are never stagnant. We are either moving toward each other or away from each other. That movement is change. But movement is only growth if the movement we feel is toward each other. Movement away from your spouse is definitely change, but it is not growth. It might encourage growth, spur growth, but the movement itself is not growth.

How do we grow in our marriage? There are a lot of ways couples seek growth in their marriage, some more effective than others. Here are a few examples:

- Spending time together is huge, but we have to be careful how we use that time so that it will lead to growth. Spending all your time on the couch watching movies is OK. Taking some of that time and spending it playing a game is good. Spending that time learning more about each other through conversation and open-ended questions is really good. Spending some of that time talking about spiritual things and in deep conversation is great!
- Another example is attending marriage events or conferences. Attending is good. Participating once you are there is better. Taking what you've learned and applying it to your marriage is great! Booking the next one because you saw how the experience positively impacted your marriage is awesome!
- Reading a book on marriage is OK. Reading a book on marriage together is good. Reading a book on marriage and discussing the content is great! Applying what you are learning in that book to encourage growth in your own marriage is incredible! (If you are reading this book together, having the conversations, and being consistent, you are currently doing something that will lead to growth in your marriage. Well done!)

Whether you are doing one of these things or others I haven't mentioned in detail, such as counseling, dates, growing in your relationship with Christ (which can do amazing things for your marriage), spending time with a mentor couple, attacking conflict authentically and quickly—these all nurture intentional growth in your marriage.

However, there are always two sides to the proverbial coin. Just as these activities encourage growth in various levels, there are things we do that prohibit or stunt our growth in marriage. Things like not making time for our spouse, talking negatively about our spouse to our friends or coworkers, not acknowledging our spouse's needs, ignoring conflict, and many more. These are all proven ways to ensure change will happen in our marriage, but not growth.

How are you seeking growth in your marriage? Like many things we have discussed, the desire for growth has to be an intentional aspect of your marriage. It won't just happen on its own.

The desire for growth has to be an intentional aspect of your marriage.

DIG DEEPER

Talk about it:
Think back to the following times in your relationship: when you were dating, when you first got married, and this past year. In each of these transitional times, think about the difference between change and growth:

- Where have you seen change but no growth? Think of some ways you can turn that change into growth. Having trouble? Go back to the list I mentioned above of ways to grow in your marriage. Then make a plan!
- Where have you seen growth? Take a moment to thank your spouse for intentionally tending to the needs of your marriage. It's so important to this lifelong journey!

PRAY FOR AND WITH EACH OTHER

WEEK 11

||||||||||

PRAYER

BEFORE YOU BEGIN
Take time to prepare your mind, your heart, and your space.
Be open to change; listen well and anticipate a positive experience.

START THE CONVERSATION
- What encouraged you this past week?
- What discouraged you this past week?
- What one thing can I do to help you in the week ahead?
- What are your prayer needs for the week ahead?

5-MINUTE READ-ALOUD
Ryan:

The Bible has a lot to say about prayer. From the Psalms in the Old Testament to the Lord's Prayer in Matthew 6, prayer is a crucial, personal spiritual discipline in the life of a believer.

But what does this look like in a marriage? How should you pray as a couple? When should you pray? And why should you pray in your marriage?

To answer these questions, we will look at a passage that does not speak to marriage. However, the principles from this text certainly speak to the role prayer has in our lives and in our marriages.

Colossians 1:9–14 says this:

And so, from the day we heard, we have not ceased to pray for you, asking that you may be filled with the knowledge of his will in all spiritual wisdom and understanding, so as to walk in a manner worthy of the Lord, fully pleasing to him: bearing fruit in every good work and increasing in the knowledge of God; being strengthened with all power, according to his glorious might, for all endurance and patience with joy; giving thanks to the Father, who has qualified you to share in the inheritance of the saints in light. He has delivered us from the domain of darkness and transferred us to the kingdom of his beloved Son,[4]in whom we have redemption, the forgiveness of sins.

From this I want to show you three ways that you can pray for and with your spouse.

First, you should pray with *persistence*. So often when we pray, we get so discouraged when we don't see immediate results, so we quit praying. Here, Paul was praying for his fellow believers, and he said he had not ceased praying for them. As followers of Jesus, it is never too late. Lazarus was dead and in the grave for four days, and it wasn't too late for him. No matter what we are praying for, keep praying. Don't give up. Jesus promised his followers that persistence in prayer would be rewarded, and that promise applies to us too.

Second, I would encourage you to pray with *purpose*. In verse 10, Paul told us exactly why he was praying for them: so they could walk in a manner worthy of the Lord, so that they could please God, so they could bear fruit, and so they could increase in the knowledge of God. I would encourage you to pray these things for your spouse. Surely you desire these things for them, so if you don't know exactly how or what to pray, this passage is a good model. How often do we pray just out of obligation and without purpose?

And finally, I want you to notice the *posture* of Paul's prayer. Paul was praying that his friends might pray with a posture of humility. He asked that they receive strength from God, and that they give thanks to God. He said that it was God who had qualified them. Many couples get uncomfortable when praying with their spouse, but God doesn't want perfect prayers; he just wants you, and the same is true for your spouse. Your spouse doesn't want your prayers to be perfect; they just want to pray with you.

**Your spouse doesn't want your prayers to be perfect;
they just want to pray with you.**

DIG DEEPER

Talk about it:

- How often do you pray with your spouse? Set aside a specific time daily or weekly to pray with your spouse, and make it a priority. Put a reminder in your phone if this helps you form the habit.
- Do you ever pray over your spouse? Praying over someone means God receives your prayers on their behalf. You are specifically praying for their needs. Sometimes you may be holding their hand, or resting your hand gently on them, but you are together. Ask your spouse if you may pray over them when a particular need arises, or when you sense they need this special touch of prayer, or as a regular rhythm in your prayer life together.
- Take a moment to list some things you could pray over your spouse, such as the list the apostle Paul gives us above. How might you change this list to pray more purposefully for your spouse?

PRAY FOR AND WITH EACH OTHER

WEEK 12

||||||||||

LEGACY

BEFORE YOU BEGIN
Take time to prepare your mind, your heart, and your space.
Be open to change; listen well and anticipate a positive experience.

START THE CONVERSATION
- What encouraged you this past week?
- What discouraged you this past week?
- What one thing can I do to help you in the week ahead?
- What are your prayer needs for the week ahead?

5-MINUTE READ-ALOUD

Jenny:

I remember being asked on several different occasions: where do you see yourself five years, ten years, or even fifteen years from now? I've always had difficulty answering that question. I think mostly because even five years from now seems so far away and out of my control. But those questions can be helpful, even if they are difficult to answer. Why? Because the answers to that long-term vision could help lay the groundwork *now* to set you up for the *future* you desire. See what I did there? We are now headed "back to the *future*," our theme for this final part of *The Marriage Experience* series, and our wrap-up for the entire fifty-two weeks.

Let's take that same concept of doing something *now* to prepare for your *future*, but instead of your own future, think about the future of your children, grandchildren, those that are close to you, those that see you as an inspiration, or perhaps all of the people in your mission field, wherever that may be. This is your legacy—what you leave the next generation, the mark that you leave on the world, and your own household.

Did you know that your marriage can have a major impact on your legacy? Think about how you originally learned about marriage, what it looked and felt like, its purpose, and its impact. Did you have parents who set a good example of a healthy, perhaps messy, but gospel-centered marriage? Possibly your parents weren't the greatest example, or you may have grown up in a single-parent home and not witnessed any marriage first-hand. You may have learned about marriage by another relative, parents of friends, or even from the media—television or movies.

Whether you know it or not, you brought into your own marriage the legacy of the marriages that greatly influenced you as a child. Those examples could have left a positive mark on your understanding of marriage, or a negative one. But what was left for you doesn't have to be what you leave for your children. You have control over how you act in your marriage and can therefore set a legacy that can positively impact those under your influence.

Thinking about your legacy is important because the impact you have on your family through your marriage, good or bad, will far surpass your life on earth. A bad legacy can be destructive while a good legacy can be life-giving to those who spent time with you, especially those who grew up in your home.

How is this different from one's heritage? Heritage refers to the past—your ancestors, your roots: where you came from, who you came from, your culture and traditions. Legacy is about the future, gifts given to those who come after you.

The first book of the Bible is, of course, Genesis. The word "Genesis" means origin. What came about on earth in Genesis laid the groundwork, or legacy, for those of us who followed. I think of the very beginning of sin, Adam and Eve in the garden, and the legacy that followed through painful toil and painful childbirth. But I also think of God's promise to Abraham and the legacy Abraham passed down through his faithfulness to God, not to mention his legacy of physically adding many generations, which includes you and me!

The impact you have on your family through your marriage will far surpass your life on earth.

What kind of legacy will you and your spouse together leave for this world? The marriage that you have will impact your children, your neighbors, and your community. The model that you set for those watching can and will survive you by generations. Are you mindful of that when you are making decisions? Are you mindful of that when you are communicating with each other, both through praises and conflict?

How do you leave a desirable, positive legacy through your marriage? By being open and honest in all of the aspects of marriage, not just the "good" parts. This doesn't mean airing all your dirty laundry for everyone to hear and see, but neither does it mean keeping your messy marriage locked up tight. Avoiding conflict around your children might leave a marriage legacy for them that is unattainable. When our kids see a "perfect" marriage, they might strive for that and never find it—because it doesn't really exist. Show those around you a real and authentic marriage. Show them a marriage that involves laying a *foundation* of connection, unity, humility, forgiveness, submission, respect, discipline, accountability, and encouragement, all the topics we discussed in Part One.

Demonstrate a marriage that allows you to grow closer to God and therefore to each other by being sanctified in the power of the Holy Spirit and enjoying the *fruit* of that relationship, as we learned in Part Two. Establish a marriage that is a deep, loving *friendship* (Part Three) that includes sacrifice, compassion, romance, affirmation, trust, gratitude, honesty, loyalty, and vulnerability. And by demonstrating these things, the *future* of your marriage (and theirs) will be driven by a single mission, purpose, dreams, hope, prayer, play, continued growth—and all of that will be your legacy.

If that doesn't fire you up, I don't know what will! (Cue the *Rocky* music!) Now you have a job to do. You have a legacy to leave. You are adding to that right now by working on your relationship with each other. Never stop learning about each other and working toward a healthier life together. Your spouse will thank you. Your children will thank you. Your friends will thank you. Your community will thank you. And by presenting the gospel to those around you through your marriage, God will look on you with kindness and favor because you are advancing his kingdom.

DIG DEEPER

Talk about it:

- What kind of legacy were you left when it comes to your relationships? What are some negative aspects that you might have unknowingly brought into your own marriage that need to be corrected—or removed? What are the good aspects that you hope to continue to pass on through your own legacy?

- What if tonight one or both of you were called home? Would the relationship you have with each other right now be one that you would want reflected in your children? Would it impact the next generation positively or negatively? What is one thing you feel you need to work on to ensure the legacy you leave has a positive impact on those around you?

PRAY FOR AND WITH EACH OTHER

WEEK 13

||||||||||

CELEBRATION

YOU DID IT! By the end of this week, you will have completed *all four parts* of *The Marriage Experience*. This last part has been deep, hasn't it? We had a goal of giving you an effective tool to help you build the relationship with your spouse that you desire. And, guess what? You're doing it! Now it's time to celebrate again! Remember the purpose of marriage? Let's say it again:

The purpose of marriage is to reflect the relationship that Jesus Christ has with the church.

Hopefully, now that you understand the purpose of marriage, your life has already begun to change or, as Jenny clarified a few weeks ago, to grow. If you have put in the effort to learn and grow through any of the fifty-two topics we've covered, even a little, then:

- YOUR marriage **has become** more Jesus-centered.
- YOUR marriage **has become** more gospel-centered.
- YOUR marriage **has become** more sacrificial and full of grace.

Even if you still have a lot to work on, remember, this is a process, a journey. There are no perfect marriages, no perfect spouses—only a perfect Savior.

So, how should we celebrate such an amazing accomplishment? Here are some big ideas:

- Enjoy that overnight getaway we reminded you to schedule in Week 5.
- Hold a ceremony, privately with each other or with others who are on this marriage journey alongside you. Perhaps use those vows you wrote in Week 4 to recommit yourselves to each other, or to a marriage that fulfills God's highest purpose for you as a couple. Perhaps share communion together at the end, reenact special moments from your wedding ceremony, or do something symbolic you missed when you got married.
- Go public! Have a party! Bring out the good china and prepare something special to eat! Crank up the music, push the furniture back, and dance! Toast the beautiful covenant of marriage together with other couples, or your extended family, and have some fun!

The most important thing you can do to celebrate each other is to keep growing. Keep practicing. Keep having important conversations with each other. At minimum, keep meeting at least weekly to check in, pray with each other, and communicate about the week before and the week ahead.

Now that you have been on this marriage growth track for an entire year, consider starting over again with Part One. This time, you should find it easier to have deeper conversations. Use a journal, and mark your growth as you go along. Encourage another couple to go through *The Marriage Experience*. Gift them with their own book, or lend them yours.

We are so honored you have chosen to spend this time with us. We would love to hear from you and to continue to support you in your marriage journey. Stay connected through our website or send an email to contact@the-marriage-experience.com. Please share your honest feedback here and wherever you purchased this book. Through your input we can continue developing effective tools to support you and others on this wonderful, messy, gospel-centered marriage journey.

PRAY FOR AND WITH EACH OTHER

INHERITANCE

HAVE YOU EVER LOST a family member, and then learned that you received an inheritance from them, perhaps a favorite object, a piece of furniture, or a sum of money? The idea of an inheritance is referred to often in the Bible, with Scripture often giving us reason to have hope for the future, which of course is our theme for Part Four of *The Marriage Experience*.

In Week 7 we talked about *hope* and asked the following question:

> If your spouse has a relationship with God through Jesus Christ, do you view them as someone who has eternal hope and has received an inheritance from God?

Perhaps one or both of you do not feel you have that eternal hope, or that inheritance from God that comes when we accept Jesus Christ as our Lord and Savior. If not, then all you have just been through in *The Marriage Experience* was leading you to this moment. You can have the most important conversation of your life, right now, with God himself. The book of Romans gives us an easy way to understand what God requires of us. Let's look at a few key verses, beginning with Romans 3:21–25:

> But now the righteousness of God has been manifested apart from the law, although the Law and the Prophets bear witness to it- the righteousness of God through faith in Jesus Christ for all who believe. For there is no distinction: **for all have sinned and fall short of the glory of God,** and are justified by his grace as a gift, through the redemption that is in Christ Jesus,[5] whom God put forward as a propitiation by his blood, to be received by faith.

Keep reading! You will soon find Romans 6:23, which says, "**For the**

wages of sin is death, but the free gift of God is eternal life in Christ Jesus our Lord.”

Now let me ask you about inheritance. If someone wants to give you an inheritance but you refuse to accept it, is it yours? No! Just like any gift, it doesn't belong to you unless you *accept* it. And, of course, you cannot accept it after you yourself pass away, can you? It's the same with God. He is offering you the gift of eternal life, paid for by the blood of his own Son, Jesus, for your sins, and for ours. All he requires is that we *accept* this free gift.

If you have never done this, if you have never talked to God about this, now is the time. Let him know that you realize you are not perfect and will never be able to "earn" your way into heaven. Express your realization that Jesus was his Son, and came to earth to pay the price for your sins. Then, let him know that you accept this amazing inheritance, the free gift of eternal life with Jesus Christ as your Savior. While you are having this conversation with God, ask Jesus to be Lord of your life. Put him in charge. When you do, you will experience an amazing inner peace, and something else: hope!

If you just had this conversation with God, please, let us know right away. We want to help you take the next step in your faith journey. If you have more questions, we want to hear from you. Write to us at:

contact@the-marriage-experience.com

RECOMMENDED READING

Chasing Perfect: Peace and Purpose in the Exhausting Pursuit of Something Better, Alisha Illian

Designed to Lead, Eric Geiger and Kevin Peck

Forgiving What You Can't Forget, Lysa TerKeurst

Love and Respect, Dr. Emerson Eggerich

Mere Christianity, C. S. Lewis

The Advantage, Patrick Lencioni

The Five Love Languages, Gary Chapman

The Meaning of Marriage, Tim and Kathy Keller

You and Me Forever: Marriage in Light of Eternity, Francis Chan and Lisa Chan

ABOUT THE AUTHORS

RYAN AND JENNY BROWN have a love for marriage and a longing to give married couples a space to connect on a deeper level in their relationship. They created *The Marriage Experience* as a biblical approach to creating a strong, gospel-centered marriage, the result of ongoing prayer, biblical study, and research, along with their years mentoring newly engaged and married couples.

The Marriage Experience project's ultimate mission is to help couples illuminate Jesus Christ to the world, in keeping with Ephesians 5:32. The-Marriage-Experience.com is an online community for couples in any stage of marriage looking for support and encouragement in deepening their relationship.

Ryan is Executive Pastor of Gatherings at Graceland Church in New Albany, Indiana, where he has served since 2013. He received his bachelor of science degree in business management from Indiana University Kelley School of Business, Bloomington, Indiana, and his master of arts in church ministry from Southern Baptist Theological Seminary, Louisville, Kentucky. Ryan's experience spans the spectrum of ministry through his pastoral service with youth, small group, discipleship, preaching, evangelism, outreach, worship, and administration, yet he would say his heart and calling are to lead and shepherd the local church. Ryan cheers for the Indiana Hoosiers, the Indianapolis Colts, and the St. Louis Cardinals. He collects sneakers, loves to read, and enjoys coaching his son's soccer team.

Jenny is director of *The Marriage Experience* ministry, the result of her passion for encouraging and supporting women and strengthening marriages. She is also the creator of *Simple Life, Pastor's Wife*, an inspiring online platform and faith community of women encouraging one another to live a Christ-centered life beautifully, simply, and inexpensively. Jenny is a frequent podcast host and interviewer. She received her bachelor of arts degree in telecommunications from Indiana University, Bloomington, Indiana, and her master of arts in education from Lipscomb University, Nashville, Tennessee. She taught for nine years before becoming a "stay-at-home-mompreneur." Jenny serves alongside Ryan at Graceland Church as she manages her online platforms and their marriage ministry. She is very comfortable with a power tool in her hand and always has a building project in mind.

Ryan and Jenny were married in 2004 and have two children. Contact Ryan and Jenny at:

contact@the-marriage-experience.com

ᴛʜᴇMARRIAGE
EXPERIENCE

MORE IN *THE MARRIAGE EXPERIENCE* SERIES

THIS BOOK IS DESIGNED to build each part on the previous section. Be sure to experience them in order. Each is also available as a stand-alone eBook download.

Part One: Foundations
Part Two: Fruit
Part Three: Friendship
Part Four: Future

The Marriage Experience 52-week softcover and eBook
    ISBN 978-1-7343231-4-6
The Marriage Experience 52-week hardcover
    ISBN 978-1-7343231-1-5

Published by: Encourage Publishing, New Albany, Indiana
                              www.encouragepublishing.com

Find *The Marriage Experience* series through your favorite reading app, through the publisher at www.shop.encouragebooks.com, anywhere you like to purchase your books, or through the *Marriage Experience* community website.

WHAT OTHERS ARE SAYING

"The Marriage Experience *by Ryan and Jenny Brown is a powerful yet user-friendly tool that can heal and strengthen any marriage. In it, Ryan and Jenny do a phenomenal job of guiding conversations for couples that address biblical topics with wisdom and practical advice—allowing couples to dig deep and grow in their marriage together in a safe and helpful way. If someone is wanting to transform their marriage from one of the world into a relationship that mimics Christ and his bride—the church—then look no further than* The Marriage Experience."

Quinn Kelly, licensed Marriage and Family Therapist,
Creator of sanctificationandspitup.com blog and podcast

"The Marriage Experience *is an absolute game-changer. Whether you are happy, hurt, or ready to hang it up, Ryan and Jenny have created a simple and powerful tool to help couples strengthen their relationship, communicate effectively, and experience intimacy in a God-ordained way. This is a much-needed framework for engaging and productive conversations that can heal and encourage every marriage.*"

Alisha Illian, author of *Chasing Perfect*
Founder of Women [re]Purposed

"*A great marriage is a warm friendship, clad in a coat of love, trimmed with a scarf of romance. But how do we get there? Through* The Marriage Experience. *I've never seen anything like this material. It's simple, practical, biblical, and doable. It's as down-to-earth as a weekly date, and as simple as reading, asking, listening, and loving. Nothing complicated about it. You can't walk through these pages without emerging into a more enviable marriage. Whether you're newlyweds or young-at-hearts, say, 'I do' to* The Marriage Experience."

Robert J. Morgan, author, speaker, Bible teacher, pastor
www.robertjmorgan.com

"*Ryan and Jenny Brown are committed to healthy marriages that display the gospel to the world, and this book is a product of that commitment. This is not simply a book to read. It is a conversation guide, designed to lead a couple into both discussion and action. The topics are well chosen, the text is to the point, and the questions are framed to lead the couple to talk about things that every couple should discuss. I recommend this book to any couple seeking to strengthen their marriage.*"

Zane Pratt, vice president, Assessment/Deployment and Training
International Mission Board, Southern Baptist Convention

"*Ryan and Jenny Brown have been lifelong friends and their marriage has always been an example of trust, communication, and intentional love. This book perfectly sheds light on the beauty marriage unveils with commitment and trust in the Lord. With so many marriages failing around us, this book is exactly what we need. The Browns have perfectly laid out an easy way to connect with our spouse and take the intentional time to build a lasting marriage. I am so excited to have something written from both perspectives, of husband and wife. To be able to take in both viewpoints and then be able to focus on my marriage and apply the teachings is a gift. Well done!*"

Rachel Van Kluyve, author and podcast host of *She Made Herself a Home*
designer and creator of www.crateandcottage.com

JOIN *THE MARRIAGE EXPERIENCE* COMMUNITY

Do you have a marriage that leaves a lot to be desired?

Are you connecting the way you used to or like you want?

Perhaps you are searching for a way to build trust and lay a foundation of safe communication within your marriage.

That's why we created The Marriage Experience community: tools and resources to help you navigate life's most rewarding partnership: the one you have with your spouse.

- Resources
- Inspiration
- Connection
- Encouragement

contact@the-marriage-experience.com
www.the-marriage-experience.com

ENDNOTES

[1]Warren, Rick, 1954-. The Purpose-Driven Life : What on Earth Am I Here for? Grand Rapids, Mich. :Zondervan, 2002.

[2]Chan, Francis, Lisa Chan. You and Me Forever: Marriage in Light of Eternity. San Francisco, CA. Claire Love Publishing 2014

[3]Hornby, Albert S, Michael Ashby, and Sally Wehmeier. Oxford Advanced Learner's Dictionary of Current English. Oxford: Oxford University Press, 2000. Accessed 4/20/2022, https://www.oxfordlearnersdictionaries.com/us/definition/american_english/respect_1

[4]Illian, Alisha. Chasing Perfect: Peace and Purpose in the Exhausting Pursuit of Something Better. Eugene, OR. Harvest House Publishers 2020.

[5]Lennon, John. Lyrics to "All You Need is Love." Performed by The Beatles, EMI Studios, 1967. *Genius,* genius.com/The-beatles-all-you-need-is-love-lyrics

[6]Marshall, Penny. A League of Their Own. Columbia Pictures, 1992.

[7]Keller, Tim, Kathy Keller. The Meaning of Marriage: Facing the Complexities of Commitment with the Wisdom of God. New York. Penguin Random House 2011.

[8]River Valley Worship. Lyrics to "Hope Has a Name." Performed by River Valley Worship, Million Lifetimes, BEC Recordings, 2018. Rivervalleyworship.org.

[9]Keller, Tim, Kathy Keller. The Meaning of Marriage: Facing the Complexities of Commitment with the Wisdom of God. New York. Penguin Random House 2011.